THE

POWER

OF YOU!

**NO ONE IS YOU,
AND THAT IS YOUR POWER!**

BERTINA POWER

S.H.E. PUBLISHING, LLC

The POWER of You! Copyright © 2022 by Bertina Power.

For information contact: **www.shepublishingllc.com**
www.BertinaPower.com

Cover and Title Page Design by Michelle Phillips of CHELLD3 3D VISUALIZATION AND DESIGN

ISBN: 978-1-953163-37-0

First Edition: March 2022

10 9 8 7 6 5 4 3 2 1

DEDICATION

*This book is dedicated to my two heartbeats, my legacy, Brandon and Haydon. For without them, I would not have been able to define my purpose, which ignited my passion within, and now I am stepping into my **POWER**.*

FOREWORD

POWER. People kill for it. Men die for it. Soldiers go to war over it. Many will do whatever it takes to get it. We engage in a struggle to obtain it. The word is mentioned over 260 times in the Bible. It is the by-product of money and influence. It is the hottest of commodities; an abstract concept that manifests through circumstance. It is the most coveted entity known to man, and yet, most have no clue how to get it, or what it really is...until now!

I do not believe this an accident that you made a conscious and deliberate decision to purchase this book entitled *The POWER of You!* You, like me, have an inner craving to know what **POWER** truly is, what it feels like to have it, and what it takes to obtain it. You want the secret sauce that adds flavor to the way you move through this roller coaster ride called life. A sauce so thick, rich, and well-seasoned that folks will come from far and wide just to taste it. A sauce so life-altering that it will keep them coming back for more.

Well, Eureka, you've struck gold! That secret sauce will no longer be a secret after reading this book. I will provide this warning, though. It may not be the recipe for **POWER** that you may be expecting. The kind of **POWER** here is not the type that starts wars or incites violence. It does not pit human against human, feeding the faulty notion that we must kill each other to acquire it. The idea is not to use it to hurt or harm or be instrumental in bloody takeovers.

No, this is about a **POWER** that builds, uplifts, gives life, and strengthens spirits. This kind of **POWER** is designed to bring focus and clarity, rather than chaos and confusion. It is not found externally initially, but it originates inward then shows up through results that manifest on the outside. This **POWER** is irreplaceable and priceless, with the capacity to catapult you to your next dimension of success. It leads to self-mastery, which is the highest, strongest form of **POWER** that exists. It leads to lasting change originating from your internal self.

As an educator, the **POWER of Activation** and the **POWER of Mindset** mentioned here have enhanced the way that I teach and relate to my students. As an author and speaker, I have learned how to use the **POWER of Words** to paint on beautiful canvases for my readers that allow them to see the words in pictures. As the founder of a non-profit organization, the **POWER of Resources** reminds me that there is always a way to get what I need, if I just remain focused on the solution and follow through. As a mother, the **POWER of Prayer** and **POWER of Forgiveness** have been invaluable tools to create a space for spiritual coverage, love, and peace for not only my children, but my entire family. This book has been nothing short of a blessing and indispensable source of **POWER** and information for myself and those with whom I have shared it.

I would like to invite you on a journey as we explore the many facets of true **POWER**. I will be right there with you as this amazing author pours into us all. I am continually becoming and overcoming in small increments each day, surprising myself with the plethora of creative ways that I can use the **POWER**s mentioned herein. My deepest desire for you is that by the time you read the last word, you will feel your **POWER** so deeply within you that you will hardly be able to contain it. I pray that *The POWER of You!* settles in the depths of your mind, heart, soul, and spirit for the remainder of your days. May it be a magnet that attracts all those who find themselves in your presence, and a light unto your path.

Peace and Blessings,

Lesa

"Personal POWER is something that is not visible.

We can see its effects, but we cannot see POWER itself.

In the same way, we see the effects of wind,

but we cannot see the wind."

~*Frederick Lenz*

CONTENTS

THE

POWER

OF YOU!

NO ONE IS YOU,
AND THAT IS YOUR POWER!

BERTINA POWER

INTRODUCTION

"Mamaaaaa, it's a boy!" These were the infamous words spoken by a precocious 2-year-old with hard-bottom walking shoes after discovering the gender of her brand-new baby brother. This mini ball of fire came into the world on a lovely Easter Sunday, a burst of energy that hit the scene on the Southside of Chicago. "Who *is* this child?" seemed to be the question of the day whenever any adult was around her for more than a few minutes, as not many knew quite what to make of her.

First-born child of a regional library director and high school chemistry teacher, she soon showed the world that she was no ordinary addition to the Earth's population. This was evident by her stomping into the infant ward as a toddler demanding that the nurse "give me my baby" so that her baby brother could be taken home from the hospital. Of course, she perplexed the adults in the neonatal unit when she revealed that she knew that her baby brother was a boy because "boys have penises and girls have vaginas." You see, as the first born, her mother had been preparing to share the spotlight. If they only knew this was just the beginning.

As the years progressed, it became obvious that a star was born. She was amongst the top of her elementary, high school classes, and later a Magna Cum Laude graduate of her beloved Hampton University in just three years. This dynamic young woman had a future so bright you needed sunglasses to protect your eyes. Yes, she was making a grand entrance into the real world, and she was ready to take it over.

Eventually, life's tour took her to Connecticut, New Jersey, and New York. She had a blast in New York modeling, and over time adopted the New York accent and tough exterior that we associate with being a Native New Yorker. Described as tall and statuesque, with a deep, sensual voice, this **POWER**house commanded immediate attention upon entering any room. The world was at her fingertips, and she aimed to crack open that oyster and gain all its treasures. Armed with a strong, solid family foundation, eagle eye, sharp mind, and accounting degree to fall back on, she had all the bases covered. Her first job in finance in Connecticut was the result of building a foundation with her accounting degree.

Soon, life in all of her unpredictability moved chess pieces around and made a boss move. The winds began to howl fiercely, lifting Dorothy off the ground, twisting her violently through the air, and plopped her down right back home in Chicago. Her return was not under the greatest of circumstances, but this girl knew how to take life's lemons and make chocolate cake. Does it seem impossible to produce cake from lemons? Exactly, but this is what she specialized in, turning the impossible into possibilities. Real estate became her noun and selling became her verb. She fell in love, got married, and had two babies. Entrepreneurship also became a part of her life when she opened her very own franchise real estate office. Everything was playing out like a fairytale, until it didn't.

Do you remember the 2007-2008 housing market downturn? If not, it is worth researching. Although I will not go into detail about it here, suffice it to say that it left an indelible mark on our country's financial history. Housing prices plummeted and property values were all but nothing. The real estate world suffered immensely, especially those who had acquired properties prior to the downturn, losing both their money and real estate investments. Since no one was selling or buying properties at the time, there was little to no need for real estate agents, loan officers, appraisers, and others involved in the real estate game. The effects were crippling, and she was one of those real estate professionals adversely affected.

Within a few years, after the dust settled, she found herself the divorced, single parent of a preschool-aged son and infant with severe disabilities, a business that had gone belly up in the wake of the market crash and having to swallow her pride to live with family members. Suddenly, her entire world was turned upside down. Just imagine, a fiercely independent woman who prided herself on not having to ask anyone for anything, the object of envy and jealousy in childhood and adulthood, now standing in line at the welfare office applying for government aid. Humbling is not a strong enough word to describe that experience.

Soon the cocktail of divorce, verbal and mental abuse, the shock of giving birth to a baby with cerebral palsy, financial devastation, and family tensions began to take a toll, as they would on anyone. Depression, fatigue, suicidal thoughts, and despair crept into her spirit and mind, leading her to ask, the age-old question, "Why me?." A question like this was so counterintuitive to her positive, never-say-die, "can-do" approach to life. A natural-born problem-solver and solutionist, this lady knew how to make things happen. The reality is, sooner or later life hits all of us in the head with a brick and knocks us off our square. Nobody escapes it.

In every human experience, regardless of who you are or what you have acquired or accomplished, the road of life gets rough and bumpy. The best and most carefully laid plans go haywire and leave our vision for the future blurry and out of reach. The pain, disappointment, and heartbreak can feel unbearable, causing us to cry out for a quick fix. Inevitably, and sometimes with a funky attitude, we ask a poignant question, "What in the hell?".

Then, one day, the skies open again, and the sea stands still. The tsunami ends, restoring hope with the flood waters receding. Focus and clarity return, and we come out on the other end better than we went in. Order returns to the land, leaving evidence of an evolution and revolution that has taken place within us because of the experience. This is a beautiful picture, isn't it? The trials, tribulations, and obstacles followed by the overcoming. Sounds like something right out of an Ancient Egyptian story where victory and triumph reign after a long, tiring battle against a formidable enemy. A renaissance takes place, replacing the old and birthing the new.

Surely the ultimate win incites feelings of celebration and jubilation, that is, until *that* thought sneaks into your mind and wrecks it. Amid the restoration party, as you examine your proverbial and/or actual scars, you wonder "What was all of that for?" and "Why did it have to be so hard?", and "Why did it have to be ME?!". Seriously, we could not have reached this destination without all the hoopla and "extraness?" Was all this *necessary*? The answer, the young woman would say, is a resounding YES! It was vital. Her entire journey was essential, the good, the bad, and the ugly. How would you know there was light without darkness, and strength with no weakness? Would the spoils of war have the same meaning without the battle? Would there be as much of an appreciation for the destination if the journey were smooth? Similarly, as gospel recording artist Fantasia sings in her award-winning song, "It Was Necessary."

Life teaches lessons with varying price tags, but we all go through the checkout line at some point. No one rides the train for free; that conductor is making rounds to collect. The **POWER of Mindset** in this book illuminates the path to flipping our struggles into credits in our bank accounts of life. The struggles, when viewed from the proper perspective, produce humans with supernatural mental strength that can, as the unofficial Marine slogan states, "Improvise, Adapt and Overcome." This is what drives *The POWER of You!*

The POWER of You! cultivates, plants, and waters the seeds of success buried inside of our spirits until which time they create a harvest. That young woman, like Dorothy, was equipped all along with everything she needed to win the chess game of life and return to herself. She used her **POWER** to weather storms and sidestep the victim mentality. She wants you to know that you have unlimited potential with the tools you need to activate and harness your greatness. That woman knows that you can become unstoppable. That woman believes in you. That woman is me.

XOXO

Bertina

"**A feeling of confidence and personal POWER comes from facing challenges and overcoming them.**"

~Brian Tracy

POWER OF MINDSET

"Once your mindset changes, everything on the

outside will change along with it."

~ Steve Maraboli

I n every person's life, there is a pivotal moment when everything changes. There is a microscopic snippet in time that represents the line of distinction between the former and the latter, the old and the new, and the past and the present. The second that you realize that the way that you see the world and yourself within it will never be the same. In this space, you process every situation, circumstance, and event that occurs in your life through a lens that did not exist before. This is the instant the mind shifts. This is the manifestation of the **POWER of Mindset.**

There is no force more **POWER**ful than the human mind. It is what makes us unique as individuals. It is one of the entities that separates us from the animals. What the human mind can do through sheer force of will is nothing short of miraculous. It is what kept POWs alive for years in conditions that we could not begin to fathom. It is the force that gives mothers the strength to lift cars off their babies. It is also this force that can determine if a hope will live or if it will become a dream deferred.

Mind vs. Brain

Discussion surrounding mindset would be not complete without mentioning the mind and the brain. Though there is a tendency to use these terms interchangeably, they are not the same. The mind, according to Merriam Webster.com, refers to "the element of a person that enables them to be aware of the world and their experiences, to think, to feel; the faculty of consciousness and thought." Included is also a simpler definition "...the part of a person that reasons, feels, understands, and remembers." Notice the repeated use of the word "feels."

Now let us look at the brain. The brain is described as "an organ of soft nervous tissue in the skull of vertebrates... the organ that is responsible for the processing of thoughts." The Mayfield Clinic further expounds upon this definition by stating that "the brain assembles the messages in a way that has meaning for us and can store that information in our memories. The brain controls the execution of our thoughts, memory, and speech..." If you look at the descriptions of both the brain and the amygdala, you will see that while they complement one another, they serve different purposes.

Have you ever seen those encyclopedia-type pictures of the brain that both fascinate and repulse you? Well, that wrinkly muscle is the executive that administrates the affairs of the entire body. It is the HMIC (Head Muscle In Charge). Housed within that locus of control are two key components of the brain responsible for our mindset: the amygdala and the hippocampus.

The amygdala is the section of the brain that processes fear, stress, and anxiety. When a person experiences these feelings and emotions, the amygdala is activated and lights up like a Christmas tree. Are you familiar with the terms fight or flight? The amygdala is where the decision to fight or flee originates. This directly connects with the **POWER of Mindset** because within it lies the **POWER** of decision.

In the previous section we became acquainted with the amygdala, the interceptor of all things fear and stress. The amygdala is directly connected, both literally and figuratively, to a part of the brain called the hippocampus. No, the hippocampus is not a species of large mammal that spends lazy days hanging out by the watering whole soaking up the sun on the African Savannah. The hippocampus is the feeder for the information and events received by the amygdala. Responsible for memory formation, the hippocampus functions like the old school Dewey Decimal System and determines how information received from the amygdala will be categorized. Now let's further link this to the **POWER of Mindset**.

Bertina, why are we talking about the amygdala and the hippocampus? These may sound like terms you studied in your undergraduate course "The Human Brain and You." What in the world do these things have to do with mastering the courage to launch a business, transitioning to the next level in my career, or convincing myself that I can start that podcast? It has everything to do with it.

Come and go with me on a journey. Close your eyes (yes, I do realize that you will have to stop reading). Ask your mind to recollect a time when you wanted an opportunity to pan out so desperately that you were sure your nerves and anxiety were going to eat you alive. For me, this was right before I gave my first speech as Student Council president to the student body. For you, it may have been your very first job opportunity, getting married, or running for a coveted office or position. Do you remember the internal dialogue that went on inside of your head in the moments leading up to the event? The conversation may have gone something like this:

"I've waited a long time for this chance. Years of volunteering, traveling, serving on committees, paying dues...I have put in my time and now I am ready and willing. I am excited, but honestly, I sure hope it doesn't turn out like last time. I was ready then, too, but things didn't quite turn out the way I expected. All that time spent campaigning, preparing speeches, passing out fliers, and Susie Sunshine STILL got the position. How crushing! Sigh, maybe this isn't such a great idea. I cannot bear to go through that humiliation again. Maybe I should wait."

Read the internal dialogue one more time. Let it sink in. What do you notice? Do you see the line of demarcation in this thought? Initially, the inner talk was hopeful and confident. We were our own hype man, giving all the reasons why we were the right person for the job, including all the work and time spent in preparation. We solidly affirmed that we were capable, prepared, and up to the task. Then there was a shift. Do you see it in the next few lines? Clearly doubt, uncertainty, and comparison have set in. These dream killers have hacked the mind and seized control over this thought process. The door to limiting beliefs has been opened.

What do you think happens next? We begin to experience the emotional and physiological effects of our inner dialogue. Our unspoken words initially speak life into our impending victory, then suddenly begin to utter silent words of death. We move from highlights to hindrance, from conviction to disbelief, and from clarity to ambiguity. Where our confidence stood tall and strong like a redwood tree, it now droops and leans over like a weeping willow. In the course of about four minutes, we have totally derailed the massive self-assurance that was housed within our core and sent the train speeding toward a crash and burn.

How does this happen? What makes a person go from holding pom poms and cheering at their own victory game to becoming a spectator in the crowd leading the "booing" section? It's all about the connections. No, not the networking kind of connections, but the connections made between the amygdala and hippocampus during similar past experiences. These connections boss the mind around and tell it how it is *supposed* to feel about these experiences.

You see, when humans have any type of experience, the hippocampus decides how that event will be remembered and classified. Let's say, for example, that you are taking a nice, leisurely stroll through the park one warm and sunny afternoon. Suddenly, to your surprise, you look up and come almost face to face with a beautiful deer. You are on foot and have never come within this close of a proximity with a "wild" animal before. In that micro-moment, you are startled and afraid, not knowing how this creature will react to you standing in its space. It is just you and she, female to female (unless, of course, you are a male reading this). Your heart is racing, and your first instinct is to run, but your feet will not move, so you just stare. Finally, after what feels like an eternity, the amazing creature turns and gracefully glides away in the other direction. You breathe a sigh of relief and high tail it back to the safety of your car.

Now, let us examine this situation from the standpoint of the parts of the human brain. You are walking along and are surprised by the deer. In this case, fear is the automatic response because you have just encountered the unfamiliar: you have never been this close to a deer before in such a vulnerable, open space. Feelings of vulnerability and unfamiliarity trigger stress and fear in the human body. Remember, we learned in an earlier section that the amygdala is the part of the brain that receives and processes stress, fear, and anxiety, and that the amygdala feds directly into the hippocampus, which, in turn, will decide what label we are going to put on this event that has just taken place.

The most important concept, or liberating truth, of this section is to remember that despite the thoughts, feelings, and emotions provoked by a particular event, or type of event, they can be altered. This is what neuroscientists have termed neuroplasticity. Neuroplasticity describes the process by which the brain can rewire and retrain itself to think new thoughts and adopt new habits. This capacity to retrain itself is vital to the **POWER of Mindset** in that it leads to the deletion of the "stinkin thinkin" that blocks the path to our goals and dreams, and leads to a liberating truth.

Michael Hyatt discusses in his book *Your Best Year Ever* truths and beliefs can either be limiting or liberating. Limiting beliefs hinder growth and impede progress, while liberating beliefs improve circumstances and lead to advancement. There is **POWER** in your beliefs. What you *believe* to be true becomes what you expect, and your actions will soon follow. As you read further, you will learn that you can upgrade your beliefs, even if you think it's impossible. The late, great Muhammad Ali stated that "Impossible is not a fact. It's an opinion."

Anchors and Threats

In my experience as a model, real estate professional, contractor, director of education, mom, and sorority president, I have had plenty of knockdown, drag out fights with the anchors that I will be mentioning in this chapter. These anchors, or threats, are present in everyone's life in one form or another, but the **POWER of Mindset** will put them in check.

I realize that the use of the word anchor to signify a threat to our mindset may seem strange, so I will explain what I mean. The Cambridge Dictionary describes an anchor as a verb meaning "to make something or someone stay in one position by fastening him, her, or it firmly..." It also defines it as a noun this way, "any of various devices dropped by a chain, cable, or rope...for preventing or restricting the motion of a vessel..." Just take a moment to re-read that and take it all in.

The types of anchors we are referring to as they relate to the **POWER of Mindset** are the distractions that hinder our success and purpose. These anchors weigh us down, cause distractions, and throw us off course. These anchors insidiously make us forget what we are supposed to be doing and why we are supposed to be doing it. These anchors threaten our dreams, purpose, and destiny by slowing the completion process. They hold us where we are, instead of allowing progression to take place. We find ourselves stuck in our current position with growth and development stunted, if not halted altogether. All of these are a huge problem if our plan is to use our **POWER** to grab success.

Throughout my journey, I have found five major anchors that have shown up as distractions to varying degrees. We will address them from the least to greatest from my perspective. It is important to note that this ranking is reflective of how greatly they have affected me. Your life experiences may place them in a different order.

At the risk of sounding like Letterman's countdown, here is number five: society-at-large. One of the biggest threats to achieving your goals are societal expectations. The world has certain fixed expectations for the general population: go to school, then college, get married, get an excellent job, have a baby, then retire and move to Florida. Unfortunately, it does not allow for a little concept we like to call freedom of choice. What if I don't want to go to college? How about starting a business instead of getting a job? As far as children, can we explore the possibility that I just want to donate to a foundation to help feed them overseas?

Friends, number four, can be a major source of distraction along our path to success. Be honest, how many times have you sat down at your computer, with an entire plan and schedule on deck, with coffee and muffin next to you, then the phone rings? Of course, we have the option to ignore the call, double down on our task, and make real progress, but who really makes *that* choice? Let's say we make it past the first round of temptation and send the call to voicemail. Now here comes the follow-up text giving the details about the call that you didn't answer. Once you see what it was supposed to be about, your curiosity is piqued because you really do want to know what happened at the staff Christmas party you missed. "I'm going to just call really quick. Just talking long enough to find out what happened and that's it, no longer than 10 minutes, tops." That was at 6:30. It is now 7:45 and you're just getting into the details on your "quick" call. See how that happened? Can't relate? Maybe it's just me.. or maybe not.

This is a focus killer! It may be helpful to send out a message prior to the start of your work or study session to let everyone know that you will be unavailable for a designated period. This way, friends will know not to contact you unless it is an emergency. Ideally, your request will be honored and there will be no contact initiated during this time. Inevitably, someone is going to breach your request. If that happens, it will be up to you to use discipline to ignore the call. What would be wise, though, is to take note of who honors your request and who does not. That speaks volumes about people's true intentions toward you and how much they value and respect you and your time. You will find a suggestion in the chapter entitled **"POWER of Self-Care"** regarding what to do once those individuals reveal themselves. At a certain point, you realize success is a decision, and it lies within your hands.

In the number three spot I have selected, family. To be clear, I am referring to those loved ones that reside outside of your house, which pose a different type of distraction than those who reside with you daily. This dissimilarity is due to a different level of access. When family members residing outside of your home want your attention, you have wiggle room there to ignore or postpone engagement, should you choose to. You can send the call to voicemail, opt to answer the text later, or simply ignore social media until you have completed your task. When dealing with family, you need to gauge the seriousness of the matter and ask yourself these questions: 1) Is it a true emergency? 2) Does it have anything to do with me? and 3) Is there anything I can do about it right now? Based upon the answers to these questions, you can then assess if the situation requires your immediate attention and is urgent enough for you to allow it to derail your focus.

Coming in at number two are the "threats," or anchors inside of your house. As you might imagine, this gets tricky.

Children, spouses, siblings, parents, and even pets all command your attention, and quite frankly, do not always give a damn what you might be doing when they need you. Whatever is going on cannot wait, and the world will cease to spin on its axis if you do not lend immediate attention to their plight. Dinner, homework, paper cuts, missing ties, caretaking of parents, all present states of emergency regardless of the time crunch you may find yourself in. Can you guess what your best friends are in these cases? Boundaries and schedules.

Boundaries are pivotal to your self-care and focus. You must establish them yourself and then make them clear to those around you so that your expectations are understood. For instance, if you have a home office and do most of your work there, you may want to establish a rule in your home that when that door is closed, you are unavailable. Another way to establish a boundary is to delegate tasks. Let's say for example, you are in real estate and are working on a bid to buy a property for rehab. You know that the competition will be fierce, so you need to fully concentrate on your proposal. It is nearing dinner time and the natives are getting restless. Perhaps you can delegate the task to your spouse or an older child to make dinner for the evening, or maybe you can order a healthy meal from your favorite restaurant. In other words, your "not right now" game needs to be strong if you want to maintain your focus and move toward success.

Scheduling is the other piece to neutralizing the threat inside of your house. Schedules are like oxygen, and we need them to live. My daily calendar is necessary for me to function, and if it is not in there, it doesn't exist. There are times when I am asked to participate in events, attend meetings, view properties, and other things, and the first thing that I do is pull up my calendar to check my availability. If you are having a tough time finding time and opportunity to concentrate and focus on important tasks, try scheduling time specifically for that purpose. You may even want to post it in the kitchen or other community space in the house where everyone can see it. This way, all are aware of what is happening and when, and it will be known when you are working and unavailable.

Drumroll please...The number one threat is YOU! If you are anything like me, you are your own biggest distraction and worst enemy. You allow yourself to become disrupted and thrown off by the smallest things, especially when the undertaking is less than pleasurable. The phone calls that I suggested you ignore, you answer them. The text messages, you respond to. The non-emergency "emergencies" that curiously seem to come up every time you sit down to work, like the missing right shoe or black and gold tie, you deal with instead of delegate. These are situations that you have the **POWER** to manage in a way that maintains your focus, yet so many of us jump at the opportunity to search for the almond butter in the pantry, instead of appointing someone else to do it. Why? The truth is that sometimes we subconsciously want to be distracted.

Did that last statement ruffle your feathers? If so, that's good. That was my intent. This is something that messes people up repeatedly, myself included. Procrastination, anxiety, doubt, disbelief, all of these will lead us to create distractions where there are none. Case in point: you are completing your business plan to submit to the SBA for the loan for which you are applying. You are under the wire, and the clock is saying tick tock. It is due in 48 hours, and you can feel the time slipping away. It is natural to want to take a break, so that you can return with fresh eyes, so you decide to go into the kitchen to prepare a cup of coffee. This is a necessary act of self-care. Well, guess what else is in the kitchen besides the coffee maker? You guessed it, a television!

You glance at it once, then twice, then chuck it to the wind and turn it on. After all, the news is important, right? Every responsible adult should watch the news at least once a day to find out what is going on in the world around him. Wait a minute, hold on. When you first turn on the TV, you are quickly reminded that it's not just a TV. It is also the internet, which then gives the option to connect to Netflix. You look at the clock, and think, "Hey, I've been working for four hours straight. I read in a blog that the brain needs periodic breaks from thinking." So, you click on Netflix, and before you know it, it is 3 hours later because you are binge-watching Season 4 of your favorite show. Now it's 2 a.m. and you are too tired to focus. You just sabotaged yourself in a major way. No one called, came over, sent a text, or sent subliminal messages through your computer to throw you off your square. You did that all by yourself. Sound familiar?

My Story

Transparency. There is no way that I could produce a work discussing the **POWER of Mindset** without sharing my own story, at least in part. The authenticity of this entire book rests upon the implementation of all these **POWERs** in my own life, which is how I can tell you that they work. As a child, most things came easy to me, as I was a natural scholar and ambitious person. I was social, outgoing, and popular, with an amazing circle of friends and associates. At home I was a model child and older sibling that received a tremendous amount of support from her parents. My home was financially and emotionally stable. I had a good life.

As you read in the introduction, I began the young adult leg of this journey with all the promise in the world. Shortly after college, I worked as an auditor, modeled, and lived the big city life. I traveled to places like Paris and London, and had a wonderful time. I discovered new skills and talents, unleashed them on the world, and loved every minute of it. It was the ride of a lifetime, that is, until I moved back home. This is where the story takes a bit of a twist. This is when *The POWER of You!* began to materialize and take over.

Upon relocating back home, a series of interesting events took place. I worked a while for a financial institution, which re-ignited my interest in real estate. Real estate is where I really cut my teeth in sales and realized that I had a knack for it. I had also fulfilled my dream of becoming a member of an extraordinary sorority, of which my mother and several relatives were also members. This, of course, gave membership an even more special meaning. Eventually, I got married, our first pregnancy ended in a miscarriage, then we had our first son, who was breech and born via C-section. Things were going quite well, and I was living the dream. Little did I know that the life I was living was quiet before the tornado.

Suddenly, it seemed as if my life was tossed up into the air, spun around several times, and landed somewhere outside of Kansas. The real estate market crashed, and I lost everything. Within a period of just a few years, my second pregnancy ended in an emergency C-section in which both my son and I almost lost our lives. In fact, he wasn't technically alive at birth. The doctors had to work on him for 10 minutes and were able to revive him. The result was my newborn baby being permanently disabled for the rest of his life. At the time, I had no clue as to the level of care that this child would require, and what it would necessitate of me emotionally, spiritually, and physically. In processing this information, bear in mind that I also had a preschool aged child at home.

As if the distressing news of his condition was not enough, I had to fight with the hospital staff's limited belief that he would perish right there in the NICU within 3-6 months. My liberating truth, however, did not allow me to believe what the doctors and nurses were telling me to be facts. I believed that there was a purpose for his life, or the 10 minutes spent reviving him would have been to no avail. The family meeting with the doctors is where I was told of the severity of his disability, which sent me into a catatonic state of shock. Clearly, none of these people knew what mama they were dealing with. There was no way in hell I was going to just throw in the towel because someone else said so and give up on my baby. Never!

After 28 days in the NICU, my baby and I went home to get settled in. I soon realized that I was not prepared for the realities of what I was about to face. My husband offered little to no emotional and physical support, and admittedly I was in over my head regarding care outside of the hospital setting. Apparently, I did not factor in things like eating, rest, caring for my other son, and self-care when I decided to go against the grain and take my child home. I was a champion for a while, pushing through the utter fatigue and exhaustion that made me delirious. What blind-sided me even more was the depression and suicidal thoughts that crept up like a grey shadow tapping me on my shoulder, appearing as an uninvited guest. These were anchors that converted my liberating truths into limited beliefs, causing me to question whether I could actually do this.

As you recall, by the time I had my first son, I had already experienced verbal and emotional abuse in my marriage and financial ruin. I had also put all of my resources into a new office that I fought long and hard to open up, and then I had to close it as quickly as I opened it. I was just beginning to get settled in that office when the crash hit. Gone. The properties I was brokering deals on? Gone. My condominium that I worked so hard to purchase for my family? Gone. After several years of trying to save my marriage, it ended in divorce. I soon found myself living with my family, struggling to take care of a preschooler and an infant with special needs with no job and no money. Have you broken out the violin yet?

Oh, but don't cry for me Argentina! This is not a book about doom and gloom. Here is where the story gets good. This is the part where I tell you all about putting my big girl panties on and making things happen. Right here is where *The POWER of You!* kicks in and turns the tables. I pulled from everything that I have ever learned, mustered all my strength and reserves, reanimated that girl that made things happen, and took control of my thoughts. It would require all these things to pull myself out of the rabbit hole. With God's grace, favor, and mercy, I knew that it could be done. It HAD to be done, and I HAD to be the one to do it.

POWER Moves

The **POWER of Resources** chapter will go into more detail regarding **POWER** moves that I made to begin changing my situation, but in this chapter, I will focus on the **POWER of Mindset.** I knew that the only way out of my predicament was to first get a handle on the way that my mind was perceiving and processing what was happening. I knew that if I allowed the darkness to overshadow me and seize my thought patterns, I would be done, and by default, so would my children. It was critical that I force my mind to bend to my will and do what I told it to do. In other words, I had to control it, I could not allow it to take the wheel and drive us into an abyss. If I didn't control it, it was going to control me.

So, what did taking the wheel look like? It involved viewing the situation in a whole different light. I had to ask myself a hard, but necessary question, "Bertina, who's driving this car, now? Make a decision so we can move accordingly." The first thing I had to do was DECIDE and CHOOSE to exercise the **POWER** within me. Had I not done that, it is highly unlikely that I would have made it out of that black hole. The point I want to drive home in this section is that the **POWER of Mindset** begins with a definite and deliberate decision to achieve a clear goal. With it, you can pull yourself out of any situation, over time and with help, no matter how challenging or difficult it may be.

From there, I began to disrupt and interrupt negative thought patterns, including the desire to commit suicide. This fight was mental, and since I had always been a fighter, I was ready for it all. My mind was the battlefield and *The POWER of You!* was the weapon. I learned early in life that if negative thoughts are permitted to take root, they will grow like weeds and destroy everything. There is no **POWER** in that! Exhaustion was met with a jolt of strength. Perceptions of my son as a burden flipped to blessings and gratitude. I chose to see the emotional and financial stress that weighed so heavily on me as a chance to flex the **POWER of Resources**. One such resource was therapy, which included medication and talking things through with a professional about my fears and challenges. It was through these conversations that I was reminded to put my mask on first so that I could help myself, and then help others. I became more **POWER**ful with each **POWER** move!

This was the **POWER of Mindset** and *The POWER of You!* at play. These experiences tested my strength and resolve in a major way, yet I was able to make it through to the other side. In the end, it propelled me. My trials were the springboard that landed me in a position to see life through the lens of a trial-tested overcomer, rather than a defeated victim. Instead of remaining derailed, distracted, and depressed, I emerged clear, focused, and victorious.

This is my message to you. If you do not grab hold of any other lessons in this book, I want you to remember this. Life's storms come to water the seeds of your purpose. Take the dirt thrown on top of you, add nutrients to it, and allow it to become fertilizer for your dreams, goals, and ambitions. Take those bricks thrown at your face and build with them, one by one. Remember that there is **POWER** in adversity. You have the **POWER** to run through walls and accomplish what you will. Adversity, obstacles, and setbacks provide excellent opportunities for growth and development as you learn to solve issues and become more resourceful. This is *The POWER of You!*

Final Thought:

"Difficulties do not come to destroy you, they come to help you realize your hidden potential and ***POWER.****"*
~Bertina Power

POWER Points

☞ **You have the POWER to force your mind to bend to your will. Bend it!**

☞ **You control your thoughts and responses. Control them!**

☞ **With great risk comes great reward. Risk it!**

No one is YOU, and that is your POWER!

POWER OF PURPOSE AND PASSION

"Purpose is how you use your experiences, talents, and gifts to better the lives of those around you."

~ Lindsay Peterson

We need purpose. *I* need purpose. I believe in it strongly and strive to live each day in its pursuit. I see living without it as being all dressed up with no place to go. It is your "why" for existing. It gives you a reason to get out of bed every morning. It drives you and pushes you when you feel like you have nothing left in the tank except fumes. Its absence sentences you to a less than fulfilled life, which can lead to the dangerous question "Why should I continue to be here?" There have been thousands of quotes, books, blogs, and memes created around it. People have spent entire lifetimes in pursuit of it. Purpose is critical to human existence. Without it, I could have been taken out a long time ago.

What does purpose bring?

Purpose brings good fruit into our lives. The first is **order**. When you know your reason for being, there is a rhythm and a rhyme to your movements. Rather than doing things in a haphazard, chaotic way, your course of action is deliberate and aligns with your end goal, which is your purpose. The Bible says that "the steps of a righteous man are ordered by the Lord" (Psalms 37:23). While I am not here to determine righteousness or advocate belief in any religion, the message of this verse is germane to this topic; when walking in one's purpose steps (actions, choices, activities) are orderly and clear. This is the only way that I can live. My true belief is that if your "why" doesn't make you cry, it's not big enough!

Purpose brings **hope**. Hope is the belief that more is coming, with the confidence that what is coming is better than what is and what was. Hope is that intangible thing that keeps us dreaming and planning for the future, even when we do not necessarily trust in it on the highest level. Hope is what gave me the chutzpah (pronounced hootspa), or extreme confidence and audacity that I needed to take my child home with me from the hospital when everyone around said that his life would be over as quickly as it started. Hope led to faith, which led to movement. Today, my child is in the double digits! A mindset of hope helped me to defy the odds.

I realized that my baby was my purpose, and that purpose, in turn, gave me a reason to turn the tables on adversity. Hope also gave me the presence of mind to tap into the **POWER of Resources** to rebuild from my broken pieces after losing what felt like everything.

Purpose brings *strength.* The setbacks and obstacles that you will inevitably face as you move through this world make you stronger when you are chasing purpose. Chasing purpose builds stamina and endurance. It develops character and creates a force to be reckoned with. When you fall down, and we all fall down, and want to stay down, it screams at you to get your ass up and keep moving forward! Strength says, "No retreat, no surrender!"

Finding Purpose

Every single living being has a purpose and the **POWER** to find it. No one is born without a purpose. Sometimes a mentor or coach is needed to flesh it out, but it is always there. As a trainer, mentor, friend, and trusted confidant, I have been asked to assist others with finding theirs. While I am not the Oracle, my passion and purpose for helping others realize their full potential and **POWER** has put me in the position to successfully assist in this area.

Self-reflection and engagement with others have revealed to me that your purpose is likely something that you have already been engaging in on some level. I think that sometimes we expect purpose to present itself in some grandiose way, like in the form of a lightning bolt or booming voice from heaven, giving step-by-step instructions regarding how to achieve it. A letter written in invisible ink appearing on your doorstep is a good way to find out your purpose, in the movies. Well, life is not a movie and we live in reality. You will have to manifest *The POWER of You!* to realize your purpose, and you can do it! Here is something to think about.

What is your passion? Something that you do for the sheer joy of it, whether you get paid or not. What do you do in the service of others that also brings you happiness? Answering these questions is an additional means by which to figure out your purpose. Let me give you an example. A woman has been struggling with finding purpose for years. She has stated repeatedly that she feels lost, confused, and hopeless because she cannot seem to identify her life's purpose (remember we identified hope as one of the things that purpose provides). She shares that writing poetry, teaching Sunday School, and tutoring youth are all activities she has enjoyed and have done effortlessly. Do you see a common thread in the responses? Teaching, writing, children, and youth are all mentioned. When asked how long she had been performing these types of activities, she shared that she had been doing them in some form since childhood. She was living her purpose the entire time and did not realize it.

My life is no exception. I have always been a service-oriented, extroverted, outgoing, people person. Beginning at the age of two when I demanded that the nurse "give me my baby", it was apparent that I had the **POWER of Presence** and commanded attention upon entering a space. In fact, my mother could not bear to leave me alone in the backyard for fear that I would run up to a stranger and start a conversation. In high school, I held various positions that required me to speak publicly and perform acts of service. My voice and height have always paved a way for my purpose wherever I went, however, in my mind these two things have always been my Achilles heel. Steve Harvey said, "Your gift will make room for you. Quit running away from it!"

As stated before, people have trusted my counsel for years, knowing that I have the capacity to bypass emotionalism to arrive at sound advice. All these qualities converge to form my purpose: to em**POWER**, inspire, educate, and serve. If you look closely, you will see evidence of all these in the work that I have done.

The **POWER of Purpose** can also show up in a third way. The seemingly never-ending cycle of challenges, tests, and trials that appear up in your life are uniquely designed just for you, like an exquisitely custom-made suit or fur coat. The areas where you are lacking, especially in character, will constantly be tried and tested. At this writing, I am immediately reminded of my level-up period with patience. As I mentioned earlier, I grossly underestimated the amount and level of care that my son would require as a special needs child. Honestly, at the outset I did not want to own that I was on the patience "struggle bus", and the driver was not letting me off when I pulled the cord. Patience had never been my strong suit, and I was accustomed to movin' and shakin' to my own beat, doing things how and when I wanted.

After bringing him home from the hospital, I received the shock of my life. Not only could I not continue to march to the beat of my own drummer, but there were also times when that brother had to put the sticks down altogether. This became evident when moving with my two sons. My oldest son could move independently, whereas my youngest could not. Every action had to be performed for him, except for breathing and blinking. The option to just grab his hand, throw a diaper bag over my shoulder, and tell him to come on and get in the car was not on the table. Extreme patience was required. The experience was, and still is, humbling and demanding, but grew me in an area that was critical to my future success. Without it, my purpose walk would not be as purposeful or **POWER**ful!

Purpose and Passion

I love my life and what I do. I make no apologies for living life full out, fearlessly, and out loud. People are always asking me how I do it. Where is the fountain that I get my limitless energy supply from? Want to know the secret? Purpose and passion. Purpose and passion are like my two best friends, life-long partners that can't stand to be apart. Each can stand alone but will never be as effective individually as they will together. The relationship between them is symbiotic, they feed on one another and need each other to survive. It reminds me of the closeness that I share with my oldest son.

When it comes to conjoining purpose and passion, it sparks the question of whether the chicken or the egg comes first. Does purpose give rise to passion, or is passion required to step into your purpose? Merriam-Webster.com says that passion is "a strong level of enthusiasm or excitement for something or about doing something." So, does identifying and choosing to walk in your purpose create the excitement, or does the gusto felt for a particular gift or talent identify it as your purpose? As for my answer, I believe that it can be purposely passionate and passionately purposeful. As for yourself, your life's direction will lead you to your own answer.

Regardless of the answer that you arrive at to the above question, authentically fulfilling your purpose will require many things, especially passion. Passion gives you the drive to finish the race when you want to stop twelve steps from the finish line. Passion is fire that begins as a flame. The raging heat of passion must be so intense that it can be felt for miles. True passion is an inferno that no amount of water can extinguish. If you allow the process to unfold, your passion will push you to your purpose and enhance the experience incredibly. The key is the desire and will to allow it to happen. You have the **POWER** to wed the two together in a wonderful ceremony that will make you **POWER**ful beyond measure.

My Story

My son's birth gave me unwavering patience and a passion for children with special needs. I never in my wildest dreams would have imagined being in that position, but it was a huge blessing in the end. It sparked something in me that I didn't know existed and one of my purposes was revealed, which was to bring to the forefront awareness of individuals with disabilities and special needs. I have volunteered and fundraised for the March of Dimes for years as they were an intrical part of being in the NICU providing mothers with education and various services.

I recently joined a luxury global real estate firm who partners with the Special Olympics and became the representative for our local offices. In this role, I am responsible for involving our agents, staff, family, friends, and community leaders in the movement. Also, in 2017, I started a scholarship endowment fund in my son's name to assist those with special needs in reaching their higher educational goals. Inspiring and motivating others to go higher and achieve more is a *purpose* fulfilled by my gift and **POWER of Presence.**

Are you feeling passionate about your purpose after reading this chapter? I hope the answer is a resounding YES! Never doubt that you have a purpose, a reason for being. Water the seed of your purpose. Allow it to grow into a strong and **POWER**ful oak tree with passion at its root, and success and accomplishment, as you define them, as its leaves. Give yourself the freedom to walk in your purpose. You will light the path for others to do the same! My all-time favorite quote by Marianne Wilson from the movie *Akeelah and the Bee* states, "and as we let our light shine, we unconsciously give other people permission to do the same."

Final Thought:
Each of us has a purpose.
Pursue your purpose with passion!

POWER Points

☞ **Purpose brings order, hope, and strength. Walk in it!**

☞ **Purpose gives you a reason to keep going. Keep pushing!**

☞ **Our purpose is not for us, it is to be used in the service of others. Serve!**

☞ **Passion is the fire that fuels your purpose. Ignite it!**

No one is YOU, and that is your POWER!

POWER OF WORDS

"Death and life are in the power of the tongue..."

~ Proverbs 18:21, King James Version Bible

"It's probably worse than you think. You should just let the baby go. Don't do anything to try to save his life. You can have more children."

As long as I have breath, I will never forget these words. It was not until they hit my ears during one of the most traumatic moments of my life that I had a true understanding of the **POWER** and impact of words. I felt them in the pits of my soul. They cut right through me. These words from my father, the one I turned to for empathy and understanding, took me completely by surprise. The way that I felt when I heard these words made it clear that words can shatter your soul or uplift your spirits, thereby giving them tremendous **POWER**.

Words are **POWER**ful, invisible, colorless entities with the destructive potential of a nuclear bomb. Words can construct or destruct, edify or perplex, unify or separate. They can elevate a person to the highest of heights, and then in an instant sink the same person deep into an abyss. Words have the capacity to fill one with love or hate, hope or despair, courage or fear. Words can mend a heart or break one. Words, like fire, can warm a home or burn it down.

Sometimes words play in your head. Sometimes they exit your lips. Words cause things to become manifested into reality, both positively and negatively. They are directly linked to the **POWER of Activation**. Words encompass how you speak to yourself and what you say to others. They dance the tango with perspective. They are conveyed through written and spoken tone and communicated through body language. Sometimes words are unspoken, and scream louder than what is said. This is why I find the **POWER of Words** so fascinating.

I am captivated by words and the **POWER** they possess. I should be dubbed the "Quote Queen" since I have them written down all over the place. Words are everywhere, spoken and unspoken. They are interwoven throughout everything that I do, from training to working with clients. I have had to master them in order to be successful as a speaker, real estate professional, and educator. I have seen first hand the difference they make concerning the outcome of a situation and how others are affected by them.

Words and Connection

Words have a direct connection to the brain. Once they have been released into the atmosphere and connected, the **POWER of Activation** begins to bring them to life. In other words, they are potent enough to have the same effect on our minds, hearts, spirits, and bodies as physical actions do. Words penetrate the subconscious and live there, filed away until something happens to trigger them back to the surface. This is why, according to attendees at my training classes and speaking events, I have been successful in this area. "As usual, energetic, motivational, and inspirational", and "The best class ever in 16 years of business and motivation..." are examples of the responses received from attendees. I don't share this to brag, but to demonstrate the **POWER of Words**.

To dive further into this explanation, I will refer to the amygdala and hippocampus that we learned about in the **POWER of Mindset**. Do you recall the role the amygdala plays in the network of the brain? Of course, you do! That's right, it's the part of the brain that lights up when we feel fear, stress, anger, or anxiety. As a quick side note, did you smile when I affirmed you by saying "Of course, you do?!" THAT was the **POWER of Words** in action. Now, I'm going to let you in on a little secret. The exact same neon lights illuminate in the brain when you hear or see something that causes fear or anxiety as when there is an action that results in these responses. Surprised? This is the **POWER of Words**.

Now, allow me to shed further light on this topic. When we have positive and pleasurable experiences our bodies release feel-good chemicals. Have you noticed that when someone of significance gives you a compliment, or you nail a speech or presentation, you feel a rush? How about when you are physically or intellectually aroused? Do you feel as if you are on a natural "high"? Believe me, I have felt it a few thousand times. It's that feeling like you are floating on air. The reason that you feel high is because you *are* in a sense. You feel this sensation because the same chemicals secreted when individuals are in a state of "traditional" high are the same ones released when we have other favorable experiences. The "feel great chemicals" endorphins, dopamine, and serotonin show up in both cases.

This is why words are so important. The way you speak to you, whether those words are audible or spoken internally, have the deepest and most profound effect upon your psyche. It is natural to focus on what others do and say to us, especially since we are trained from childhood to teach us that a good, active listener is one that pays close attention to the external voices. I was trained this way. How often, though, were we taught to listen to that soft, still voice that resides within? That's the voice that is with us all day, every day.

The fact of the matter is our inner voice has such massive **POWER** that it can make or break an outcome. This is when we have to use the **POWER of Mindset** to control the words in our head. Why, because as the popular saying goes, thoughts create both audible and inaudible words, which are directly linked to actions. Proof positive of this is clear when I think back to the day in that hospital room when I heard those life-changing words concerning my newborn son's diagnosis.

"You the mama, you the mama, you the mama" were the words that I eventually spoke to myself to gain control of my state of mind upon hearing the news concerning my son's prognosis. Reminding myself that *I* was this child's mother and therefore it was my responsibility to bend this situation to my will, was the only way I could snap myself out of it. Three words, so simple, yet infinitely **POWER**ful. Without them, the tragic prophecy spoken over my son's life could have easily been fulfilled. Later, the words "Let me tell you what we finna do now," is what I said to the hospital staff that was trying to tell me how we would proceed regarding my son. This sent a clear message that I was not about to just accept what I was told without question. For the record, after 28 days in the hospital I did walk out of there with my son in tow. Defying what I was told, with the **POWER** of my tongue, was the deciding factor in the outcome.

I was conscious of the **POWER of Words** very early on. Growing up the child of a library director and high school chemistry teacher, I *thought* that I understood just how **POWER**ful words were. I mean really, can you imagine how much reading and speaking was required as not only a top student in my class, but Student Council President and underclassmen mentor? Have you ever been in a position where you were required to lead by either your words or actions? I was a visible force both in school and out, constantly using words to express myself. In addition, as the oldest of four children, mother expected me to use my words to speak life and motivation into my younger siblings. I knew that although I did not apply for the job, my inherent task was to be a role model and inspirer for all three of them. I am proud to say, they all turned out awesome!

Using the POWER of Words

One of my many TV moments on the Steve Harvey Show was an opportunity to use the **POWER of Words** in front of millions of viewers. Certainly, as I stood there exercising the **POWER of Presence** looking stunning in my pink and pearls, the **POWER** of my voice and words is what ultimately made the event timeless and momentous. "Steve, what do you think I should do with this voice?" was the question I asked that day. You see, I was not asking Steve to affirm me. That's not why I was there. I was there to use my **POWER of Resources** to solicit feedback from a trusted source regarding ways to maximize the benefits of my gift. My question clearly conveyed to Steve, the studio audience, and myself that I already knew that this gift would be of great benefit to my life and the lives of others. I was simply requesting advice regarding the vehicles by which I could maximize those benefits.

Most recently, I have been blessed to have remarkable opportunities to use the **POWER of Words** to help others access their **POWER** in my role as a teacher and trainer. Word choice, delivery technique, and timing have all played a central role in my effectiveness over the years. In addition, I bring an infectious energy (according to attendees) that makes people want to zero in on my presentations. This, no doubt, is why I was chosen to appear on several HGTV shows and flex my real estate muscles before the world!

One of the biggest lessons that I have learned concerning the **POWER of Words** is to keep my treasures and accomplishments close to my heart. Have you ever had to learn the hard way that not everyone is happy for you and cheering you on the way that you might think? Sometimes the very ones that you share the most with are the same ones who will sabotage you behind your back. This then causes you to change your mindset. If you adopt this shift in thought and become quieter and more reflective, the words that you do not say concerning your situations are made up for you. When I operate in this mindset, all types of speculation and made-up stories about my life and affairs begin circulating. Such is the nature of humans, what you won't tell, they tell themselves. In short, as an unknown author stated, "Keep your next move to yourself."

Wisdom and Words

A final word on the **POWER of Words**: this **POWER** necessitates the use of wisdom. Dictionary.com defines wisdom as "knowledge of what is true or right coupled with just judgment as to action." Merriam-Webster dictionary describes wisdom as "knowledge of what is proper or reasonable." In fact, wisdom is so important that the Bible dedicates the entire book of Proverbs to it.

Wisdom is also the correct application of knowledge acquired through life experience and then using sound judgment to apply it. To put it plainly and connect it to our discussion, do not speak unless you know what you are talking about and have something to back it up. Monitor what you say, as well as hold back when it is not appropriate nor prudent to say anything. Wisdom is not just knowing what to say, but also what *not* to say. In addition, it is knowing who to say what to, and when to say it. Timing is incredibly important, as the right thing said at the wrong time can be just as damaging as the wrong thing at the wrong time, and the wrong thing at the right time. This is one that everyone thinks they get right.

One thing about the use and timing of words, like most things in life, is that no one is perfect and there is always room for improvement. No matter how diligent the effort to "watch our words", they get the best of us at times. We will not always use our words to provide information, ask for resources, inspire, or motivate. There will be times when we make a misstep in their use. We will falter, we will embarrass ourselves, and we will inevitably put our foot in our mouths. This is the imperfection of humankind. Here is where the **POWER of Forgiveness** and the **POWER of Prayer** enter. If you are on the receiving end of words that cause negative feelings, you may pray or meditate on the situation and possibly elect to forgive the other party. If you are the giver, prayer for peace and self-forgiveness may be in order. Whichever you choose, allow your words to heal and emPOWER!

Final Thought:

*Wisdom of the right words can be **POWER**ful. You have the capacity to make amazing things happen using them.*

POWER Points

☞ **Words are POWERful. Use them wisely!**

☞ **Keep your words positive. Erase the negativity!**

☞ **Words have the POWER to create. Manifest something great!**

No one is YOU, and that is your POWER!

POWER OF ACTIVATION

"Each of us has a gift or talent. We must individually tap into it in order to activate it."

~ Bertina Power

D o you remember Hannah Barbera's Wonder Twins from the Saturday morning cartoons shows? For those whose memory may be a little fuzzy, the Wonder Twins were an extraterrestrial brother and sister team with amazing super**POWER**s. Though they each had individual **POWER**s, these super abilities could not be activated until the duo connected their fists, touched, and agreed, then shouted, "Wonder Twin powers, activate!" Once this ceremonial event had taken place, their magnificent capabilities were unleashed, and the dynamic duo was ready to save the world. You see, though each twin was endowed with individual **POWER**s that were a part of their DNA, it was only when the **POWER**s were galvanized that they were able to manifest.

Just like the Wonder Twins, I firmly believe that individualized gifts and talents have been downloaded into each of us. These gifts and talents, when stoked by the fire of passion, result in amazing opportunities. This notion is supported in the King James version of the Bible, specifically in Proverbs 18:16, which states "A man's gift maketh room for him, and bringeth him before great men." Steve Harvey also spoke to this when he said, "Everyone has a gift, and your gift is your **POWER**." Our gifts are valuable treasures that should be protected fiercely. The caveat to this is that the gifts that are given are only usable if awakened and stirred.

Have you ever tried driving a car without starting it up first? I mean just jumping right on in, smashing on the brake, and attempting to switch the gears, all without putting the key into the ignition. At that moment, you look over and notice the most critical component of this entire endeavor, the key, sitting on the passenger seat right next to you. Of course, you pick the key up, put it into the ignition, and now the car is ready to go. If you leave the key on the seat, no one is going anywhere. You have to put in the effort to pick up the key, then take the initiative to properly position it to maximize its effectiveness.

The second that you turned that key and started the

engine you used the **POWER of Activation**. What is activation and how is it used? In chemistry, an activator is a substance used as a catalyst. A catalyst is a chemical used to cause or speed up a chemical reaction. A *person* who is an activator inspires and motivates others to get things done, either for the activator or themselves. When using the **POWER of Activation**, one recognizes the capacity of a catalyst to propel him forward, then moves accordingly. The catalyst, or activator, awakens the gifts, talents, and abilities within, priming the holder for execution.

We mentioned earlier that the stirring up of gifts is necessary for activation. The interesting thing about gifts is that while they are wonderful and positive per se, they can also be the very things that you or others perceive to be the worst things about you. Now you may be thinking, "Someone may think that a gift is a dreadful thing?" My answer is resoundingly affirmative. Not everyone will view your gift as a gift, and some will even demonize it. Let's look at an example.

Activation in Action

World-renowned transformational thought leader, speaker, and author Cindy Trimm was born on the island of Bermuda. In one of her most famous lectures, she spoke of her propensity for excessive talking in her youth, both at home and at school. Trimm shared the way that she would be scolded harshly for her verbose personality, which created a distraction in the classroom. When young Trimm was within earshot of "grown folk's conversations," she would often lose the "battle of the urge" and interject her opinion into the adult conversation. Now, anyone who is familiar with traditional African culture knows that this is a sure-fire way to catch a backhand, as it is expected for a child to know and remain within his or her place. Indeed, Trimm's solid sense of her own self-worth and abilities manifested very early in her life, characterized by a garrulousness quite unusual for her age.

Now, fast forward fifty-five years. Cindy Trimm's excessive talking has made her a multi-millionaire with a net worth of over $15 million. Her unique voice and face have helped her create a writing, speaking, and publishing empire with satellite companies all over the world. Trimm's political career resulted in a senate seat in her homeland of Bermuda, which preceded the launch of Cindy Trimm Ministries, making Trimm a household name in numerous arenas. Talk about turning a pain point into a **POWER** point.

In my own experience, my height and comparatively deep voice for a female have been a constant thorn in the stem of my rose flower for decades. You would be amazed at the number of off-the-shoulder comments I received within a 24-hour period. "How's the air up there?" "Wow! How tall are you?" and "You must play basketball," are among my all-time favorites. Oh yes, we simply cannot leave out my apparent likeness to the Sesame Street character Big Bird and Popeye's girlfriend Olive Oil. Believe me when I say that there was no shortage of disparaging remarks about my height.

This brings us to my voice, the instrument of expression that has been the source of my greatest triumphs and greatest pain. I can recall the plethora of occasions that I ordered at a drive-thru, spoke with customer service agents, and answered business calls, only to be greeted with the title of "Sir." In the beginning, I was shocked and slightly offended. Surely, you see my name posted on the same screen that we are both looking at, and there is nothing masculine about that name. The more often this occurred, the more I began to wonder if this voice that I had been bequeathed with at birth was a blessing or a curse. While my self-confidence has always been pretty solid, there were times when it became tiresome. Then there were highlights like my television moments on the Steve Harvey Show and HGTV.

I will never forget that moment of activation on Steve's show. My question for him was basically this: "What can I do with such a unique voice?" Imagine the shock when his immediate suggestion was for me to consider creating my own 1-900 number! Was I offended? Absolutely not! Steve Harvey had just inadvertently complimented a characteristic of me that others had made fun of my whole life. HGTV didn't seem to mind either when they chose me to appear in several of their shows. In both instances, as stated previously, my pain became my **POWER**!

The **POWER of Activation** manifests through the synergy produced when you connect with the right people, in the right places, at the right time. Steve's show was the right place, he was the right person, and it was the right time. So was the HGTV experience. These are just two of the experiences throughout my life that have placed me in the perfect space for my gifts to be recognized and appreciated, which intensified the activation process. Divine order will sometimes place people in your path that you may never have otherwise come across. This perfect orchestration results in both parties receiving what they did not even know that they needed from the other. When your worlds collide, this orchestration produces a grand symphony that catapults you into **POWER**!

Finger on the Trigger

There can be many triggers to our activation. We can be activated by people, words, events, obstacles, or challenges. In other words, the crap that life throws at us can cause us to spring into action. For instance, the unfavorable doctor's report concerning my son and subsequent response activated the lioness inside, the lioness that basically said, "Hell no, it's not going down like that. I want to see my child. Now!" I have always been a fighter, my daddy made sure of that, but that flame turned into a towering inferno when my back was pushed up against the wall concerning my child. Now, they should have known not to mess with a momma bear and her baby! This unforeseen situation set off the **POWER of Activation** with a fury! An unknown person said, "Sometimes we don't know how strong we are until being strong is your only option."

The words and deeds of my dad and ex-husband unquestionably activated the **POWER of Forgiveness.** The words my dad spoke concerning my son cut deeply, but I knew I couldn't sit in that too long. In that moment I felt that this man who raised me did not know me at all. Nonetheless, I had to forgive. The verbal abuse from my ex-husband, coupled with the lack of emotional support when it came to caring for our newborn son under such tough circumstances, caused me to have to dig deep to find forgiveness. The **POWER**ful woman in me was able to find the strength to do it, and it has served me well.

The **POWER of Activation** also includes being an activator. It is not just about your passion being set ablaze but doing the same for others as well. It is encouraging others to reach their highest level as you simultaneously strive to achieve yours. It is allowing yourself to share your knowledge, wisdom, and understanding with someone who can benefit from it, and then that person passing it on to others. This is where the **POWER of Activation** and **POWER of Resources** converge.

Boldly stepping into a completely different arena and intentionally making yourself uncomfortable is also part of activation. In my life I have a group of fabulous friends, but none as amazing as discomfort. Discomfort is my closest friend. It serves me in the most marvelous ways. It is my ace, my ride-or-live, my right arm. We laugh, we cry, we rise, we fall together. Discomfort is my purpose partner and my envelope pusher. It keeps me up all night and, at times, makes me want to hide away and sleep the day away. How is this possible? I was waiting for you to ask.

When we are in uncomfortable or unfamiliar situations, it activates parts of the brain that haven't been used before. This kindles a fire of imagination, triggering the fight or flight mechanism in our brains and begs it to figure a way out. Always remember that the brain naturally seeks comfort and detests pain. This is because, as we learned in the **POWER of Mindset,** the brain's sole priority is to keep us alive by any means necessary. As you may have guessed, discomfort causes the brain to sense that our survival might be in jeopardy. In other words, the brain doesn't care about your feelings or emotions, only conserving your life. As a response, the brain activates and begins formulating modes of escape from the distressing situation, with the intent of removing the "threat" altogether.

Before going into that last statement more in-depth, I will link discomfort and activation. You must understand that discomfort is a major driving force of activation. Like pain, love, opposition, fear, and desire, it incites you to move and make things happen! Think about it, when you have on a pair of shoes that are fashionable but incredibly uncomfortable, what do you do? If you are like most of the population, you kick them off the first chance you get. Ladies, how about those spanks that you bought a size too small so that you can squeeze into that little black cocktail dress? My guess is that after about 5 hours of sucking it in and holding your breath as you mix and mingle, you entertain disrobing in the car while driving home. In both cases, extreme pain and discomfort elicited a response to end the perceived suffering as soon as possible.

The Incubation

Activation requires incubation before the launch. Do you remember as a child going to the museum or the zoo, and seeing the little chicks hatching under the lights? Did you notice the receptacle they were in? When in captivity baby chicks are always kept inside of an incubator, a container with the perfect environment for them to hatch safely and successfully. It is just the right temperature, not too hot, not too cold. Their atmosphere has everything needed to care for them during and immediately after birth. In fact, without the incubator the chicks would likely perish during or shortly after hatching in an artificial setting.

There is also an incubation period for purpose-driven, success-seeking humans. This is the season of pruning and shaping, of grooming and sculpting. Just as we lift weights in the gym to grow, sculpt, and tone our muscles to create the physique we desire, the same is vital to create the life that we want. The incubation before the activation provides an atmosphere conducive to yielding optimum results. It is our training ground, the place where we acquire the knowledge, skills, and tools essential to actualizing our goals. It is a period of being tried and tested to see how badly we really want what we claim to want. It begs the question, "Are you willing to do what is necessary to get where you want to go?"

No one who has dreams, goals, and plans is exempt from the incubation period that leads to activation. It varies from person to person, but the result is the same if utilized properly. For me, the time spent living with my family after moving back home was a particularly tough incubation period. Though it was agonizing at times, it served me well. I was able to use the **POWER of Resources** to reveal what I didn't know, as well as what I didn't know that I didn't know. It offered a safe environment, a familiar place to lay while I used the **POWER of Resources** to formulate a game plan for my exit. I allowed the discomfort to push me to my next phase of life, knowing that with the **POWER of Prayer**, **POWER of Patience**, and **POWER of Mindset**, there would be a favorable outcome. The discomfort was the key. Remember, discomfort is the quintessential activator.

My Story

Living with my family presented one of many invaluable incubation periods. For you, it may have been an involuntary job loss due to downsizing or health reasons. Your incubation could have been the result of a voluntary decision to take a leave of absence from your job or to end your employment completely in pursuit of your dream. Perhaps you elected to return to school for a spell to acquire new skills and information. Regardless of the form of your incubator, it is the optimal time to plan, absorb, and procure. It is a great opportunity to explore possibilities.

An internationally forced incubation period hit the Earth during the COVID-19 pandemic. People all over the globe were involuntarily sheltered-in-place inside of their own home incubator for over a year. Everything outside shut down and travel was brought to a halt, leaving the only available course of action to commune with family and focus on self. This lockdown period yielded unprecedented growth in the number of entrepreneurs in this country. Ivy League universities offered hundreds of classes for free to those seeking to expand their skill base. The country saw a significant rise in the number of business licenses processed at the state level, as well as an increase in the number of for-profit and non-for-profit tax identification numbers distributed. While the pandemic included an exceptionally horrid turn of events, it created space for a mass incubation leading to activation. Therein lies its beauty.

No matter how you employ the **POWER of Activation,** whom or what is your catalyst, and what your incubation chamber looks like, you have the **POWER** to make it work for you. Let it breathe in your life, take up residence in your mind, and saturate your spirit. Take it with you everywhere, you never know when an activation moment will occur. It is a **POWER**ful energy that can transcend your gifts to another level when you least expect it. You have the **POWER** to be that activator for others. The public is waiting on you to light the flame in them that will become a firestorm of their potentiality.

Final Thought:

*Your gifts and talents are waiting patiently to be shared with the world at full capacity. Connect to your **POWER** and activate them NOW!*

POWER Points

☞ **Each person has a gift. Discover and utilize yours!**

☞ **Opportunities for activation can occur when you least expect it. Stay ready!**

☞ **You can only control what you can control. Let the rest go!**

☞ **You are an activator. Light someone's flame!**

No one is YOU, and that's your POWER!

POWER OF RESOURCES

*"When every physical and mental resource is focused, one's **POWER** to solve a problem multiplies tremendously."*

~ Norman Vincent Peale

I am not ashamed to say that the **POWER of Resources** saved my life, both literally and figuratively. I can recall building while broken, frantically trying to salvage the pieces of my life that seemed to be lying around all over the place. A brick of divorce here, a shard of glass with my youngest son's diagnosis over there, splinters of wood labeled with unemployment, verbal abuse, and non-support at my feet. It felt as though someone had just come along and thrown a Molotov cocktail right into the front window of my existence. We've all been there, and at one point I swear I just looked around and said "What the f*@#!"

That state of mind did not last very long. *The POWER of You!* resting inside of me resists stagnation and the "Woe is me" mindset. I was still thinking "What the f*@#!," but I was thinking about it and strategizing at the same time. I knew there was a way out. There is ALWAYS a way out! You must be determined and focused enough to find it. I had two babies, bills, an uncomfortable living situation, and an extraordinarily small window of time to spend wallowing in self-pity. It was time to make some things happen. It was time to start making some serious moves.

Building while broken is not easy. It's like deciding to run a 5K with a swollen ankle and shin splints. It can be messy business, especially if you give your pride and ego license to run the show. Believe me, I did not want to go down to that office and ask the state for anything, and yet, there I was, applying for assistance. I got it, too. Cash assistance, EBT, and WIC. I got everything I qualified for. All the resources that would serve to be a bridge to get me over until I was able to stabilize myself and my family, and cross over to the bank of re-establishment. See, that is the thing about resources...and bridges. They are meant to be temporary, not the end of the story. Since I could not swim at the moment, the bridge was critical for that phase of my life.

Financial, Human, and Informational Resources

During the journey leading up to this point in my life, I had to utilize three distinct types of resources: financial, human, and informational. The financial resources include the cash benefits I received from the state, as well as the food and WIC. These resources were completely and utterly essential to help me provide my children with the necessities of life at that time. The key was having to get over myself and my naturally independent nature in order to make it happen.

After the housing market crash of 2007, the subsequent closing of my franchise office, and the humongous bill racked up from the birth of my youngest son, I had accumulated a massive debt. You hear people talking about drowning in debt, well I needed a hot pink life jacket. As I opened bill after bill, I used the **POWER of Mindset** to begin searching for solutions. I knew that all problems were solvable, some just required a little more creativity. It meant starting over from scratch, but as the unknown author stated, "Starting over is not the same as never having tried."

I want to add an important note here about financial resource. People often find it difficult to speak up when this type of assistance is needed due to the stigma that has historically been attached to it. The universal message for ages has been that only losers ask for financial help, and that everyone should be able to pull themselves up by their own bootstraps. If you got yourself into the mess, you should be able to get yourself out. The embarrassment and shame that this ideology evokes, in my opinion, is counter productive and diminishes one's confidence and **POWER**. My viewpoint on this is simple: if you need help, ask for it! Is it up to you to determine what avenue to use to pursue your needs, but by all means pursue the avenues. Research and investigate! The resources are out there waiting for you to connect to them!

Human resources are equally as important as financial resources. Building rapport and maintaining strong relationships make it easier to call upon these resources when needed. People are far more likely to help those who offer value, or who have assisted them previously in some way. There are also kind-hearted, selfless people who will help just for the sake of helping. My family opened their doors to myself and my two boys when we needed a place to lay our heads. Others have also come through in a pinch, constantly surprising me with their generosity. A lesson I did learn was that you must ask for what you need. The squeaky wheel gets the oil, and a closed mouth doesn't get fed.

My family members were not the only human resources that I would need to employ over the years. In fact, when I took on more responsibility with my sorority, even more human resources would become critical to the function of our household. The unique circumstances surrounding the care of my son with special needs would require around-the-clock supervision. The person, or persons, providing this service would have to be skilled and experienced in this type of care, since my son had, and still has today, highly specialized needs. As hard as it was, and believe me it was hard, and still is, I eventually had to transition him into a residential nursing care facility. This way, he could receive the care he required.

I was judged harshly for practicing self-care and for making a decision that was best for not only him, but for everyone. You see, I grossly underestimated the amount of time and energy required to care for a child with my son's condition, and quickly arrived at the point of physical and mental exhaustion. Lack of sleep and malnutrition sent me on a downward spiral into depression. So deep, in fact, that I considered ending it all for myself and my children... permanently. The few people that I shared this information with were in complete and utter shock, since most viewed me as Superwoman. *Side note: that Superwoman syndrome will take you outta here very quickly. **Don't fall for it!***

Thank God I recognized that my mental and physical health were in a state of emergency and the **POWER of Self-Care** required immediate activation. I hired babysitters and nursing students to take care of the boys. I began to make trips to the spa as I had done all my adult life to relax my body and mind. I also made time to go out for meals and drinks with friends so that I could have some adult time. As I said earlier, there were many unsolicited opinions about this, but since I did not recall asking for them, they were ignored. Sometimes ***The POWER of You!*** dictates that you are okay with being judged and criticized by those who have no idea what it is like to walk in your shoes. You may think that self-care is impossible and others may tell you it shouldn't or can't be done in situations like this. However, as Muhammad Ali said, "Impossible is not a fact, it's an opinion."

During this time period, I stepped into the role of president of the largest graduate chapter of my sorority in the Chicagoland area. Anyone who has been president of any group, let alone a Greek-letter organization, knows how demanding and time-consuming it can be. It is an unpaid gig, strictly volunteer, and you often find yourself doing 1,000 jobs within the framework of your own job description, as well as that of superior officers. There is meeting upon meeting, event after event, and trip after trip. You can probably imagine how difficult this would be without tapping into the **POWER of Resources**. I am pleased to say that utilizing this **POWER** afforded me the opportunity to have a successful run as the 50th president of my chapter!

The third resource is information. If you educate yourself in your chosen area, and put in time to do the research, you will be astounded at what you will accomplish. You are the machine. You are the thinktank. You have the **POWER** to access whatever is required to resolve your situation and make the necessary connections. Remember, always use the **POWER of Words** to ask for what you need. Your phone, iPad, computer, and local library are informational fountains for you if you would just tap into them. In the era of search engines, YouTube, Instagram, Podcasts, and plain old-fashioned books, current information is more accessible than at any other point in history. There are **NO EXCUSES!** You can use the **POWER of Resources** to find out whatever you need to know. When I hear people say they have no way of finding out how to do something, I call bullshit!

I recall one afternoon I was wrestling with some light fixtures in my new condo and called to whine to my daddy that I could not figure out how to get them to stay in. His quick response was "Look, as long as you can read you can do anything." Well, that wasn't quite the response I was hoping for. Actually, I was hoping to hear something more along the lines of, "I'll be right over." It didn't pan out that way, but he was right. Access to information is everywhere and easily accessible.

Your mind is without a shadow of a doubt the greatest resource that you could possibly possess. However, it is not generally viewed as a resource. All actions begin and end with it. It is the ultimate reserve for anything you need to accomplish your objectives. Becoming skilled at harnessing the mind and **POWER of Mindset**, in conjunction with wisdom and understanding, will put you in the best possible position. I am all about positioning and repositioning. Each move that I made, every problem that I solved, and every level-up occurred as a result of using this invaluable resource.

This is the reason that I only allow energy that is **POWER**ful in my space. Energy is real and affects environments and outcomes. As a person who feeds the minds and spirits of others with my force, I have to be sure that I control the atmosphere around me. Being told many times that I am a force multiplier, the energy that I carry penetrates whatever room I walk into, thus becoming the dominant energy. If I am positive, the space is positive. If I bring negativity, the energy shifts in that direction. Therefore, I must use the **POWER of Mindset** to monitor my thoughts and always enter into a place bringing em**POWER**ment and light.

Networking is another valuable resource that I think is important to include in this section. This is a resource that I utilize constantly, especially in my real estate business. If you are interested in leveling up in your career, business, or life in general, you will need to make connections and form relationships. There is always someone who knows more than you and is willing to share their wealth of knowledge. If that person does not have what you need, he or she may be able to point you in the direction of someone who does. Networking also puts you in contact with others who share similar goals and interests, and who have the same needs that you do. Networking builds teams, and teams create successful businesses.

Focus, Follow-Up, Follow Through

As you may have guessed, I am a staunch advocate for using the **POWER of Resources** for all people, from bridges to getting through life's hiccups, to obtaining nuggets to launch or elevate one's business. You must shake every tree and overturn every rock until you find what you are looking for. It's like being the lead detective in a criminal investigation. I have used this **POWER** extensively both in my professional and personal life, so believe me when I say it works! In my experience, I have found the following three elements of this **POWER** to be tried and true means to get it all done:

Focus: Focus on the problem that needs to be solved at the moment. Develop tunnel vision and do not allow your efforts to be derailed.

Follow up: Keep calling back, emailing, and/or sending letters until you get the answers you need. It is along the same vein as PUSH: Pray until something happens. Be sure that you are clear concerning anything required on your part. **Do not let it go.** If you haven't heard anything within a reasonable amount of time, FOLLOW UP!

Follow Through: Whatever is required to reach the desired outcome, be sure to do it. Follow through to the end. Don't stop until the work is done, and you have come to some type of resolution. Whether or not you have reached the desired outcome, follow through until the end.

Final Thought:

Resources are goldmines!
Do not be afraid to ask for them and use them!

POWER Points

☞ **Do not be ashamed to say what you need. Ask for help!**

☞ **Network! Network! Network!**

☞ **Be relentless in your quest for answers and resources. Focus, Follow Up, and Follow Through!**

No one is YOU, and that is your POWER!

POWER OF PRAYER AND PATIENCE

"Prayer is the key in the morning

and the bolt in the evening."

~ Mahatma Ghandi

"Much prayer, much power. Little prayer, little power. No prayer, no power."

his is a mantra coined by the late Dr. Clay Evans, former pastor of one of the largest churches in the Chicagoland area. I am in total agreement with these words, and a firm believer in the **POWER of Prayer**. I realize that not everyone believes in prayer or its **POWER**, but I would be remiss if I did not make mention of such an essential component of my life. I have found prayer in all its forms to be an irreplaceable and pivotal force throughout my journey. It is associated with the **POWER of Mindset** and together they produce an unstoppable machine capable of withstanding life's blows.

The potency of the **Power of Prayer** and the **Power of Mindset** combined have generated a vast reservoir of strength that has carried me through the toughest times of my life. It carried me through the birth of my youngest son which could have killed us both, financial devastation, divorce, fights with forgiveness, and a host of other little gifts that life likes to leave under the Christmas tree. Prayer combined with faith also made it possible to achieve my dream and goal of purchasing my new home. The process was not a straight line, success never is, but the twists and turns forced me to tap into the **POWER of Prayer** for strength and direction. In the end, *The POWER of You!* worked, and the goal was achieved!

Dictionary.com defines prayer as "an address to God or a god in word or thought." Simply put, it is talking to whatever higher **POWER** that you believe in, if you do believe in one. This conversation can be with or without words. There is also the option of meditation. Meditation is, according to Merriam-Webster.com, "to engage in mental exercise (such as concentration on one's breathing or repetition of a mantra) for the purpose of reaching a heightened spiritual awareness." We will briefly touch on both topics in this chapter.

Prayer vs. Meditation

Prayer is practiced all over the world in one form or another. It is a lifeline to a higher **POWER** that provides comfort and peace during the most difficult times. It is a **POWER**ful act that I perform wherever I am since it can be done with or without spoken words. I have used prayer to ask for things and to unburden my mind. Praying is something anyone can do, if desired. If you would like to pray and are not sure how or what to say, I suggest that you speak to your religious advisor or use your favorite research engine to find some online that aligns with your preference.

If meditation is more in line with your belief system, it can also be done in various settings. It is important to reference meditation in this conversation for two reasons: 1) in my view it is just as important and productive as prayer, and 2) not everyone believes in prayer per se. Meditation is simply stillness, quiet reflection and clearing the mind. It is really that simple, though there are various methods used to achieve this goal. Although this is not my area of expertise, in my research I found the following site to provide great information on this subject: **https://liveanddare.com**. This site explores twenty-three different types of meditation and best practices for implementation.

"I AM" Statements

"I AM" statements are not generally considered words of prayer. However, they are proclamations that I live by. Sometimes called affirmations, there are several favorites that I speak into my life on a regular basis. "I AM blessed,

grateful, and favored", "I AM wildly successful and internationally sought after", and "I AM a resource magnet and all
that I need shall come to me", are all examples of **POWER**ful
"I AM" declarations. A financial "I AM" affirma- tion is "I AM
so happy and grateful now that I have increasing quantities
of money coming to me daily from multiple streams." An "I
AM" statement can also be something as simple as "I AM
beautiful", or "I AM loveable and I AM loved." The words you
speak may not be true YET, but the **POWER of Words** results
in manifestation. I swear by them and strongly encourage
everyone to implement them into their daily routine. Spoken
with conviction and **POWER,** these words initiate a complete
mind shift!

Prayer and Patience

Prayer and Patience together are a dynamic duo, like
purpose and passion. Together they are a **POWER** couple,
each one growing and developing the other. Prayer increases
patience, and patience improves prayer. Prayer and
meditation calm the mind and spirit, which go hand in hand
with patience since it requires calmness to be effective.

There is an old saying that patience is a virtue, and if
that is a fact, I have not always been the most virtuous
woman in that area. Historically, I moved quickly and with
intent, and I expected those around me to do the same. When
I needed something done, I wanted it done now. If there was
someplace to go, I wanted to go that second. The nature of
my profession operated on the "early bird catches the worm"
philosophy, and I was determined to catch as many as I
could.

My Story

When my youngest son was born, all of that changed. That 'early bird' worm catcher had to wait while I fed my son, got his wheelchair into the car, and then was finally able to get on the road. Patience made me take my hand off the wheel, which was a challenge since I preferred to drive my own car. I could no longer live life by my time clock. I had to let that go. Now, my movements were governed by my son's needs and patience became my guiding force. Care had to be taken in regard to all things concerning him, from feeding to transporting. Everything could not be about playing Beat the Clock. Simply put, prayer has given me new levels of **POWER** and tolerance.

Losing my business during the housing crash of 2007, then giving birth to my first son a few weeks later tested my faith and took my patience quotient to a new level. I was a problem-solver and seemed to have the **POWER** to make things happen quickly. In this case, there was nothing I could do. I couldn't make the housing market correct itself. It would take time for me to get my finances back in order. There was no money tree in the backyard. As much as I hated it, I had no other choice except to wait, plan, and pray.

When facing difficulties in my marriage, I prayed. When I felt that I lost everything, I prayed. When it appeared that my home purchase process was going left, I prayed. I pray for myself, as well as others. As a member of my sorority, I am regularly part of a collective prayer circle. In my life's experiences up until now, prayer has led to patience and understanding, both of which enhance the quality of mindset and relationships. This keeps me in the frame of mind to be as patient with myself as I am with others.

Patience is **POWER!** Prayer is **POWER!** Combined they have made me a better mother, sister, friend, and all-around person. Now I understand that not everything moves on my time, and rushing is not always necessary. Patience also increased my compassion, empathy and sympathy for others. I am grateful for the gift of patience that my son has brought into my life. It has improved the way that I mentor, train, educate, and inspire. The "big picture" is clearer now that I have learned to slow down. Patience means waiting, and waiting brings rewards. Life isn't always about the sprint. Sometimes the marathon reaps the greatest reward.

Final Thought:

Prayer, meditation, and "I AM" statements
offer a great way to center, focus, and communicate with
*yourself and higher **POWER**.*

POWER Points

☞ Prayer is a POWERful act of self-care that puts you in touch with your higher POWER. Connect!

☞ Meditation quiets the mind and binds you with your inner source of POWER. Attach!

☞ Affirmations and "I AM" statements speak POWERful words over your life. Speak!

No one is YOU, and that is your POWER!

POWER OF FORGIVENESS

"To forgive is to set a prisoner free and discover

that the prisoner was you."

~ Lewis Smedes

I am perfect. I am without flaws. I have never done anything wrong to anyone, anywhere, at any time. I am the poster child for stainless living. Is this you? Is this me? This is no one because such a person does not exist. There is no perfect person. We all err, we all fall short, we all make mistakes. Therefore, the **POWER of Forgiveness** is a perfect follow-up to the **POWER of Prayer and Patience.**

Forgiveness is a tricky word that means different things to different people. Taken from the Latin perdonare, meaning "to give completely without reservation," and the Anglo-

Saxon meaning "to pardon or overlook an offense," forgiveness has been described as divine. This is probably because it can be so difficult to do, but that's what makes it so **POWER**ful. It must be done and can be done when you tap into *The POWER of You!*

Forgiveness is an ideal that is counter-intuitive to human nature, but it is vital to success and freedom. Unforgiveness leads to holding grudges. Grudges are a 10-ton boulder sitting on your shoulders that hinder growth and make you physically and emotionally sick. It blocks blessings and sends you reeling backward, hindering forward movement. It is a dark cloud that shadows your success. There is no **POWER** to be found here.

The greatest thing is that forgiveness is in you. You are stronger than unforgiveness. Your access to the **POWER of Mindset, POWER of Prayer and Patience**, and overall **POWER of You** provides all the tools you need to step into the divine and forgive. You have the capacity to forgive not only others, but yourself as well. No matter what someone has done, be it steal a client, disrespect you in some way, or disrupt your finances, you are **POWER**ful enough to let it go and move on. You have it within you to override the default setting in your mind that sees forgiveness as a weakness. You are **POWER**ful and possess the strength of character to make it happen.

Does forgiveness dismiss accountability? Bishop Desmond Tutu in his best-selling book *"No Future Without Forgiveness,"* stated "Forgiveness does not erase accountability. Forgiveness is simply about understanding that every one of us is inherently good and inherently flawed." You see, often forgiveness is given begrudgingly or not at all because we see it as giving a "pass." We do not want to send the message that we are soft or weak, or that whatever was done is okay. In a world that upholds strength and despises weakness, that is NOT a message that is widely accepted in most arenas.

The massive size of our egos and pride also plays a part in our reluctance to want to grant it. We hold on to resentment and bitterness like a Linus blanket, not realizing that the **POWER of Forgiveness** supports our willingness to grant amnesty to that person. It is not always easy and will take work, but so does success. Just like success, it is a decision. The most difficult part is owning our role in the act that needs forgiveness. The Linus blanket feels warm and cozy when someone else is the object of the blame but starts to feel rough like wool when we are complicit.

Types of Forgiveness

First off, I do not mean to come off like I have this forgiveness thing on lockdown. I need it just as much as the next person. I have struggled with forgiveness many times in my life, but always knew that I had to figure out a way to do it. There are two types I have encountered: forgiveness of others, and forgiveness of self. In some ways forgiving myself was harder than forgiving others because I had to do some mirror work. As a rule, finding fault in others comes more effortlessly than shining the light on our own shortcomings. The best part about this is that once I accessed *The POWER of You!*, forgiveness was easy.

As I said, we've all had our struggles with forgiveness. When my youngest son was born with cerebral palsy, it was a complete shock. When we found out that he had a permanent disability and were told that he would not ever leave the hospital, the words that my daddy spoke to me will forever be etched in my brain. "Well, it's probably worse than you think. You might wanna think about letting the baby go. You can always have more children."

I'll give you a little time to process that. My dad suggested that I leave my baby in the hospital to DIE. As you might imagine, that coming from him messed me all up. I am a board-certified daddy's girl, and I would never have expected to hear that from him. I can now remember thinking, "Then you don't know me at all. There is no way I'm walking out of here without giving 1,000 percent effort." I get it, he was not pulling from the **POWER of Mindset** or **POWER of Prayer and Patience**, which would have him to seek solutions rather than allow the setback to prevail. It took me a while to learn how to access and utilize the **POWER of Forgiveness** to move past the moment.

The universe afforded me another opportunity to apply the **POWER of Forgiveness** concerning my dad. When he decided to remarry, I was not enthused, nor was I going to pretend to be. I already had a mama, the woman he married and had four children with, and I was not in need of another. No, I was not feeling that on any level. Apparently, others were able to feel it too because I was not invited to the wedding. Maybe my daddy thought I would show up wearing all black in protest or raise my hand when the officiant asked if there was anyone who objected. Whatever the reason, I did not receive an invitation, and it hurt. Again, *The POWER of You!* inside of me was activated and gave me the super**POWER** of forgiveness.

Then there is my ex-husband. The lack of emotional and physical support, as well as verbal abuse took a considerable toll on me. My entire world came crashing down around me, yet I received no help from the one person living with me who could have, and should have, been vested. My decision to forgive confused a lot of people and brought about plenty of what I call "unsolicited opinions." "Why in the world would anyone forgive someone like *that*?" The same reason someone would forgive someone like *you*," was my thought. There were several reasons that I had to forgive, all of which I won't go into here. I will say that one reason is that I firmly believe that what you put out into the universe is what you get back, and I did not want any unnecessary negativity coming my way. Another reason is that he is the father of my children. Suffice it to say, that as a strategist, I surmised that it was the best possible decision.

Self-forgiveness is just as important as forgiving others. Forgiving yourself is quite a different matter from forgiving others. It requires us to look at, and into, ourselves in a way that can make us feel uneasy. In other words, we must be willing to call out our own BS. We have to own it, ALL of it, and consider how we have contributed to the situation.

No one is exempt. I had to forgive myself for a variety of things, so I can attest to how difficult it is. In my relationship with my ex-husband, I knew prior to getting married that he had a short fuse. There were times when he exploded so quickly that it made my head spin. The pop group Ace of Base said it best when they sang "I Saw the Sign." I knew that I was walking into an inferno, but I let the pressures of society to follow the prescribed path of marriage and children cloud my judgment. Yes, I saw signs, but like millions of women and men, I CHOSE to overlook them. I repeatedly excused and rationalized away behaviors that were red flags and moved forward anyway. So, when those same behaviors showed up later, should I have been surprised? Absolutely not! Therefore, I had to forgive myself right along with him. Him for doing it, and me for allowing it to be done.

Forgiving myself was most challenging when dealing with the circumstances surrounding the birth of my youngest son. I mentioned earlier in the chapter about what my ex-husband did to mess up, but I also must acknowledge my contribution as well. When I had my first son, he was breech, so it required a routine c-section. There were no issues or incidents, all went well. When I elected to have a second child, there was no reason not to assume that things would go as well as the first time. There were no indicators of any problems throughout the pregnancy, and all appeared normal, until the very end. I was going about my usual hamster wheel life until I woke up one day and something felt "off", and it was.

What I did not know was that once you have had a c-section, each baby afterwards is delivered the same way. This meant that I should have scheduled a C-section for my second son also, but I did not. Then one day near the end of my pregnancy I woke up and noticed that something wasn't quite right. Upon arrival at the hospital an ultrasound revealed a low heart beat which I later found out was because the sac that surrounded the baby had separated from the placenta, removing the oxygen supply. My baby was suffocating, and I had no idea! By the time the emergency delivery was done, one that could have killed us both, my child was born with a permanent disability.

This was a tough one. More accurately, it was devastating! After time had passed and I reflected on the entire situation and its outcome, those self-defeating thoughts began to creep into my head. The "What Ifs" showed up. What if I had scheduled the c-section? What if I had paid more attention to my body? What if I had gone to the doctor? What if I had called 911? What if, what if, what if? These questions taunted me and would have taken me out if I allowed them to take root. I even had to forgive myself for blaming God for my son's condition. I knew that I had to employ the **POWER of Forgiveness** regarding myself, or it would tear me apart. Here I accessed the **POWER of Mindset** to prevent negative thoughts from implanting in my mind, as well as the **POWER of Forgiveness** to extend myself the same grace as I extend to others.

Benefits of Forgiveness

Anyone who knows me knows that I love information and learning new and interesting things that I can share with clients and students. For this section, I used the **POWER of Resources** to find the benefits of forgiveness. What I discovered was that there are both mental and physical benefits of forgiveness. When combined with *The POWER of*

You!, these benefits will multiply in intensity and force and create a more **POWER**ful you!

According to Johns Hopkins Medicine, there are several distinct health benefits linked to forgiveness. Among the physical benefits are lowered risk of heart attacks, improved cholesterol levels, more restful sleep, and reduced body pain. Emotional and mental advantages are decreases in depression, anxiety, and stress. I experienced all of these issues, and through therapy learned how to use self-care to overcome them. I am now a staunch advocate for self-care. The **POWER of Self-Care** can enhance the value of these benefits as they relate to overall health. This aligns perfectly with the principles of *The POWER of You!*, which promotes health and wellness as a state of being.

If the Covid-19 lockdown taught us anything it is that our physical and mental health was suffering tremendously in this country. We were pissed off, overworked, stressed out, and just plain tired. Forgiveness was part of people's healing during that time, which helped mend broken relationships and families. Unforgiveness dulls the blade of success, but when the **POWER of Forgiveness** is given full reign, it creates a bigger space for success in every area of your life.

"You can't be pitiful and POWERful at the same time. You have to choose one." This is one of the biggest lessons I have learned related to unforgiveness. Unforgiveness makes you just pitiful, literally full of pity, and mostly for yourself. That's the reason I had no choice but to forgive, because I am not interested in pity. There is nothing about *The POWER of*

You! that promotes pity parties. Sure, everyone will feel badly about something at some point, we just need to make sure that it is a brief soiree and not a gala event. The bottom line is simple: either forgive and move on, or do not forgive and remain stuck. It is either the palace or the pit, you must make the choice. As author Toure Roberts said, "You can't be weak in a **POWER**ful world."

Final Thought:

Today is the day to set your mind, body, and spirit free from unforgiveness. It is the strong that forgive, and that strong person is YOU!

POWER Points

☞ Forgiveness is not for the weak, it is for the strong. You are strong!

☞ Forgiveness sharpens your blade for success. Sharpen that blade!

☞ Forgiveness is a beautiful gift to yourself and others. Deliver the gift!

☞ Forgiveness is an ongoing process. Keep going!

No one is YOU, and that is your POWER!

POWER OF PRESENCE

"When your absence has the authority of

presence, that is power."

~ Harriet Rubin

A statement from a close friend came as a tremendous surprise but caused me to recognize the **POWER of Presence**. "When considering major decisions in my life I always ask myself, 'What would Bertina do?' I'm sure I stood there looking dumbfounded because this was news to me. It did prove what I knew to be true, and that was eyes are always watching, and ears are ever listening. There are always people whose lives are touched by their interactions with us, whether we ever know or not.

The **POWER of Presence** is a force to be reckoned with. This is felt when meeting a person with such charm and charisma that you feel the reverb of the interaction long after you have parted ways. Have you ever been in the room with a person who doesn't have to speak, the way that he carries himself says it all? Perhaps a speaker takes the microphone, says two words, and you can hear a pin drop. This is the **POWER of Presence**.

When experiencing the most trying challenge of my life to date, the birth of my youngest son, I had to dig deep and tap into the **POWER of Presence** to hold myself and my family together. The sheer weight and gravity of the situation was so great that there were moments when I just wanted to curl up into a ball and disappear. This may have been a viable option except for one thing: I knew that my oldest son was watching. What was NOT an option was allowing him to see me give up. There was no way I was going to allow him to see me fold under pressure. I would demonstrate courage under fire and grace under pressure, regardless of the realities that we faced as a family.

I paid close attention to my physical and mental presence. It would make or break the outcome and determine the quality of our future. I knew that every action taken and not taken during this time was a training ground for me to teach my oldest how to weather a storm. He needed my full presence to help him process his own questions and confusion. No matter what I was feeling, I was fully aware that I had to keep my game face on in front of him. I do want to be clear, however, I am a human and I did break down occasionally. I just did not do it where he could see.

The POWER of You! is also knowing that it is okay to have moments of weakness.

As a real estate professional, showing up is a huge part of my job. I show up to property viewings, home visits to speak with clients, and at the office to check in with colleagues and superiors to discuss the progress of ongoing projects. The **POWER of Resources**, along with the **POWER of Presence,** takes me to professional networking events. When I am present in these scenarios, I must always be spot on. Charming, alert, inquisitive, and knowledgeable, my presence gives me an edge with clients. In my field, the way that you show up is critical. People don't buy the product at the outset, they buy you. If they like you, you are guaranteed to make the sale. Keep your presence strong and **POWER**ful and you will bring in those numbers and be unforgettable!

Presence is just that important when showing up in the world. The impression you leave, especially at first contact, impacts the trajectory of the relationship or business deal. If the **POWER of Presence** is strong enough, they will purchase a product or service that they do not really need or want from you. A good presence makes you likeable, and likeability sells. This is a fact in the business world, and one of the reasons that I take the **POWER of Presence** so seriously.

Ways to Be Present

The **POWER of Presence** does not always present itself as a grand affair with pomp and circumstance. Your presence is also the way that you show up in less grandiose ways such as being attentive to your family, especially your children. I make my presence felt at my son's school by doing pop up visits occasionally just to check on him. The school staff knows me, and I make myself accessible as much as possible. Presence is also listening to the same stories over and over, regardless of how many times you've heard them.

These are **POWER**ful ways that we can be present at home. Your presence is felt by doing something as simple as sitting on the sofa with a loved one watching TV, and not saying a word. Standing in front of the refrigerator leaning against it while your significant other does the dishes or volunteering to make dinner creates a presence. These acts make a **POWER**ful and effective statement: I could be doing a thousand other things, but I choose you. There are few things that say "I love, value, and care for you" like your presence, particularly at home.

In friend groups and social circles, your presence affects the room. I see this when I arrive at dinner or a bar to hang out and enjoy time with friends and associates. "Hey Bertina, you're the MVP! It's just not the same when you're not here!" It is common for me to walk into an event and not take a seat right away due to being stopped for conversation and hugs. *The POWER of You!* is all over me when I enter any space. Perhaps you are the life of the party, the energy-bringer, the smile-initiator in your circle. That is the **POWER of Presence.**

In the professional setting, your presence is felt in the assistance that you give and talent you possess. You are an asset and **POWER**ful force within your place of business. The

Power of Presence that I bring to the workplace is like a generator that sends a volt of electricity through the building, charging everyone up. You cannot help but want to be excellent and productive when I'm in the room because of the energy that I bring, and I don't even drink coffee! I bring a natural energy and excitement with me to everything that I endeavor to do. You have the same capacity to bring the same zeal to your business environment. Just tap into the **POWER of Presence**.

As confident as I may sound regarding my presence, expressions of its effect upon people still surprise me. I was honored and stunned when I learned that a colleague had driven over an hour out of her way, rearranging her entire schedule just to attend one of my training classes. This was major, considering there was an identical one much closer to her home that she could have attended instead. In another instance, a fellow realtor stated that "...your absence is strongly felt now that you are not here. You have a powerful presence even after you are gone."

Even more surprising was walking into a ballroom filled with 2,000 of my sorority sisters for a gala event, stepping onto the stage, securing the microphone, and saying the three words "Good Evening, Sorors.", then witnessing the response. It seemed that within seconds all chatting ceased and you could hear a pin drop, and in that moment, I was not exactly sure what to make of it. Then the body language spoke volumes, it told me they were waiting for what came next. This, coupled with the response when I left the stage, made it clear that there was **POWER** in my presence that evening. This event taught me that you must know how to manage a strong presence and use influence responsibly.

I would be remiss if I did not mention the **POWER of Presence** as it pertains to ourselves. Show up for yourself the same way you show up for others. You deserve time and attention just as much as others. Put your air mask on and breathe. Take yourself out to dinner dressed to impress. Enjoy your own company, celebrate your accomplishments. This links directly to the **POWER of Self-Care**. As I have said before, I believe in self-care. I could not live without it, especially my spa treatments. It is so much easier to show up for others when you love yourself first.

Final Thought:

Your presence is a gift.
There are presents in your presence!

POWER Points

☞ Your pain points can become your POWER points. Make them work for you!

☞ You deserve to be present for yourself, as well as others. Show up for you!

☞ Someone is always watching and listening. Make your presence POWERful!

☞ The POWER of your presence opens doors. Make it strong!

No one is YOU, and that's your POWER!

POWER OF
SELF-CARE

" It is not selfish to love yourself, take care of
yourself, and make your happiness a priority.
It's necessary."

~ Mandy Hale

S elf-care is critical for all people, especially women. We take care of our families, our clothing, our cars, and even our pets. When it comes to doing the smallest things for ourselves, though, it is like pulling teeth. Well, maybe not pulling teeth since we will at least go and take care of THAT situation when it becomes painful enough. For most women, societal expectations, as well as the risk of being labeled selfish, often keep us from doing the simplest things to care for ourselves. Well, I am here to tell you that there is nothing **POWER**ful about that, and I do not subscribe to that mode of thinking.

What is Self-Care?

What exactly is self-care? I will explain by telling you what it is, and what it is not. It is recognizing and owning that you are **POWER**ful. It is taking time to rest, relax, and just breathe. It is making yourself as much of a priority as you make everyone and everything else, minus the guilt. It is knowing that you are the machine that keeps it all flowing, and that you deserve to be treated well. It is being good to you so that others will follow the expectation.

Let's talk about what self-care is *not*. It is *not* running yourself into the ground so much that people cannot tell where you end, and the dirt begins. It is *not* putting off the most basic of needs such as doctor and dentist visits, eye appointments, and hair appointments. It is *not* ignoring the fact that you are having a tough time processing through a particularly challenging time in your journey, and you may need to seek professional help. It is *not* allowing yourself to be mistreated, mishandled, or misused by anyone, not even you. Most importantly, it is *not* being willing to unnecessarily suffer through things that you would never allow someone you love to endure.

Types of Self-Care

There are a few types of self-care, but for the purposes of this endeavor we will focus on two: physical and emotional self-care. There is **POWER** in both, and they are equally important.

Physical self-care mainly pertains to care that prevents unwellness of the body and its functions. Emotional self-care, which is the sister of psychological self-care, deals with the balance of feelings and state of mind. It is important to note that while listed separately, physical and emotional/psychological self-care are intertwined. In short, whatever state your mind is in, your body will not be far behind, and vice-versa. You must listen to your body to remain **POWER**ful.

There are so many ways to practice physical self-care that there is really no excuse not to do it. For me, the spa is my refuge and guilty pleasure and getting my nails done makes me feel awesome. This is a form of self-care that both men and women can enjoy. I remember my honeymoon request to go to a spa in Arizona. We went and one of my spa treatments was a 'his and her' massage. Needless to say, he loved it and then realized why I enjoyed going so much. Taking it outdoors is another way to indulge in physical self-care. Walking, running, bike riding, and hiking are effective ways to get moving and release those feel-good chemicals that make us feel wonderful. Yoga is phenomenal, also. It is great for centering the mind and strengthening the body. Another amazing way to care for yourself is by just doing nothing! Rest and relaxation have miraculous healing **POWERs** by giving the body a chance to recover.

Equally as important is emotional self-care. As we move through the day-to-day journey of life, it is easy for our emotional state to become off balance and throw us into a state of disequilibrium. Prayer, meditation, and intentional silence are all vehicles by which a return to a balanced state can occur. Therapy is a kind of self-care that became more generally acceptable during the COVID lockdown. Talking to a professional about struggles and challenges that you may be having in your life is nothing to be ashamed of. It does not mean you are "crazy," it just means that you need a professional to help you work things out. I saw a therapist after my youngest son was born. It saved our lives and allowed me to take back my **POWER!**

The **POWER of Self-Care** also involves making tough calls about how we spend our time and with whom we spend it. People make decisions every day, sometimes without realizing it, regarding who they will interact with and who they will not. There are about 7.8 billion people in the world, and we can't possibly engage all of them. Therefore, a determination has to be made concerning who gets our time, why they get it, and how long they get it. This may sound harsh, but it is necessary, especially when you're focused, determined, and have little time to waste. Time is the most precious of commodities because it, along with life, is the only thing that cannot be replaced once it is gone. This is the reason that reflection and a little "spring cleaning" of time wasters are necessary from time to time.

You see, life is seasonal, and so are people's presence in our lives. There is a popular saying that states people come into our lives for a reason, and others for a season. In other words, all relationships are not meant to be permanent. It is not always easy to delineate between these two types of people, because they can appear to be the same. This is where tapping into the **POWER of Prayer** and the **POWER of Mindset** can be helpful. The **POWER of Prayer** connects you with the "source" that offers clarity concerning other's motives and values, as well as puts your discernment on high alert. This allows you to "see" things with your intuition that you cannot see with your physical eyes. The **POWER of Mindset** can be accessed to determine if what was discerned falls in line with the goals and objectives you have set for your life. If not, adjustments need to be made to ensure that you are walking in your **POWER**.

At times, individuals who have been in the front row of our lives need to be shifted toward the back. Conversely, there are likely those who have been in the nosebleed section that deserve a seat in the first three rows. In fact, it is highly probable that at least one person should make a guest appearance right on the stage with you. To push the point further, it may be time for the "seat fillers" in your life, the ones that you have as place holders, or random people to make the theater of your life look full, to transition to another location altogether. If this makes you uneasy, reflect on these words by Bishop TD Jakes, "What is meant to stay cannot go, and what is meant to go cannot stay."

Self-care is also saying no, which is necessary to establish and maintain boundaries. Self-care is becoming familiar with the BLOCK and DELETE options in your phone and on social media. It is making the "Ignore Call" button on your phone one of your new best friends, and not feeling guilty about it. It is also understanding that you are not obligated to answer every phone call, text message, and email that comes across your phone when it appears. You have the right and the **POWER** to decide when and where you will respond. Believe me, I have applied all of these to my life at one point or another. I exercise the **POWER of Self-Care** by cutting people off to maintain my mental health. Have you ever had to do this? It can be a painful, but necessary, act of self-love and self-care. Remember, your mind is your greatest resource and you must protect it at all costs.

As a parent, have you ever volunteered to bring treats for a school event? Well, I have and I fulfill my obligations every time. Admittedly, I have gotten some interesting looks from other parents when I walk in with my store-bought baked goods, and that's just fine. I brought them, didn't I? While I know my way around an oven pretty well, I am not standing over a hot stove baking cookies, cupcakes, or anything else when the ones at the grocery store work just fine. The students, and sometimes the parents, seem to enjoy them just the same. In these situations, I employ the **POWER of Self-Care** wisely, fulfilling my obligations while maximizing time and effort.

These principles of self-care saved me during the postpartum period after my youngest son's birth. Prior to my second pregnancy, I had been exercising self-care all of my life in one aspect or another, but now it was critical. The pressure of the situation over time had turned into self-neglect. Eating and sleeping became sporadic, and ultimately, I spiraled into a depression. At this point, I felt trapped, like the world was caving in on me and the coping skills that were once a part of my repertoire seemed to diminish by the minute. There was no way that things could continue as they were. I had to get my **POWER** back!

My mind is my **POWER** base, so protecting it was a must. As a self-proclaimed "spa-er", I began rescheduling my spa appointments. I also started to go out for drinks with friends, which provided a welcome distraction from my busy life. Interestingly, doing these things sparked a storm of criticism and judgment from others who wondered how I could leave my special needs child with someone and dare to go out and have fun. There may be times when you are judged for practicing your preferred form of self-care. Do it anyway! There is **POWER** in your self-care and since no one else is you, others don't need to understand. My thoughts on this are summed up in one of my favorite quotes: "What I must do is all that concerns me, not what people think."

Self-care became even more necessary, when my depression became so overwhelming that seeing a therapist was the only logical, responsible course of action. I swallowed my pride and sought out a good one. I will never forget the one session, which then became the second to last session, that changed the trajectory of my life. My therapist made a statement that became a mantra of mine from that day forward, which was simply, "Put your own air mask on first before you try to take care of other people." Well, how about that! What a novel idea, taking care of myself first. Just like the flight attendants always say when giving flight instructions. Well, I had been on enough planes in my life to recall this statement, however it didn't mean as much to me then as it did in that moment. It literally saved my life and the person next to me...my son. Late in 2019, I was working with a professional coach who recognized that I was still operating within my immediate family dynamics, from my toddler years. She suggested that I stop letting the two-year-old me drive the bus. This statement shattered my world too and after a good cry, I took the keys back from the toddler and began driving as a healthy, **POWER**ful adult!

COVID-19 Lockdown

The 2020 Coronavirus Lockdown, otherwise known as "The Pandemic", proved to be a blessing and a curse for many people, myself included. An unexpected outcome for me was a desperate need for rest. It was not until I experienced a forced shut down, much like the one I must do with my computer, that I realized how physically, mentally, and emotionally exhausted that I was. Have you ever experienced this? I had been going non-stop for decades chasing my dreams and caring for my two sons without noticing that I was on one big hamster wheel. On again, off again, on again, off again, constantly in a cyclical motion. The lockdown forced me off that wheel that I had been running on for most of my life and made me stop and smell the roses.

Can you relate to this? What did the lockdown do for you? It enabled me to snatch back personal self-care time. Notice that I used the word "snatch." I purposely chose this word to describe the process and mindset needed to obtain self-care time. I am now available to sleep in on a Saturday or forego meetings and events, things I would never have given myself permission to do before. Another important act of self-love that I placed into my rotation is simply popping popcorn and watching a movie with my oldest son on the weekends, allowing me the opportunity to create lasting memories. Yet, the not-so-good part of the pandemic was that I was not able to spend time with my youngest son, who was at the residential nursing care facility.

One last important point I will make regarding self-care is that it is critical for a winning mindset. Going without it in some form will have the same effect as driving a car with no oil, sooner or later it will dry up, eventually causing the engine to lock. When that happens, you aren't going anywhere! In case you didn't know, repairs for this issue are extremely expensive, but never as expensive as repairs to your mind, body, and spirit. Yes, you are **POWER**ful and want to push to make things happen, but it is so much better when you are healthy enough to enjoy the fruits of your labor. Take some time to smell the roses. Your success, however you define it, depends on it!

Final Thought:

You are the machine that keeps everything running.
Take care of it well.

POWER Points

☞ Take care of your mind, soul, body, and spirit at all costs. You only get one YOU!

☞ You cannot help someone else if you are not well. Put your mask on first!

☞ Make self-care a priority. Take care of you!

No one is YOU, and that is your POWER!

POWER OF YOU

"The question isn't who is going to let me,

it's who is going to stop me."

~ Ayn Rand

The *POWER of You!* lies in the hero that you are, a vessel willing to undergo the transformation required to become the highest version of yourself. It takes shape when you walk, and move. It permeates every aspect of your life and radiates outward. This **POWER** is transferable, creating a domino effect with each encounter. This **POWER** is multi-layered and multi-faceted, composed of many elements that culminate in a **POWER**ful and effective human.

The **POWER of Mindset** is evident in your choice to adopt a winner's mentality rather than settle for being a victim. You refuse to lose and keep getting up off the mat again and again, ready for another round. You know that there is nothing more **POWER**ful than a made-up mind that is laser focused. Fear, doubt, and disbelief are neutralized the moment they step onto the battlefield of your mind. When it comes to success, you are dressed and ready to go to war with these dream stealers at any time. This is what makes you **POWER**ful!

The **POWER of Purpose** is the alarm clock that urges you out of bed every morning to chase after your dreams. The **POWER of Passion** brings the light and heat that illuminates and warms your path to success. Passion sets your soul ablaze with an unrelenting yearning to maximize your full potential. It fills you with an intoxicating desire to fulfill your purpose. Purpose and passion are unwavering, loyal friends to the end that close the gaps of self-doubt and uncertainty. Tenacious and unflinching, the two in tandem make no concessions when it comes to propelling you to excellence. They fill you with the **POWER** to accomplish what you will!

The **POWER of Words** imparts the capacity to heal and develop yourself and others. Your words, spoken and unspoken, have the ability to create magnificent works of art in the mind and spirit. They cause opportunities to materialize from thin air, creating a space to bring your wildest dreams into fruition. They lead to closed deals and increased revenue. They turn your most em**POWER**ing thoughts into actions and habits. Your words are life-changing. Speak your **POWER**!

The **POWER of Activation** sends out a bolt of electricity, penetrating the walls of complacency and procrastination. When it senses that you are ready, willing, and able, it will dispatch a force multiplier to stand behind you and push you over the threshold. It's the jumpstart for the vehicle of your destiny and purpose, sending the **POWER** supply that makes you unstoppable. With it you can leap over hurdles and run through walls to get to your success. Plug into your **POWER**!

The **POWER of Resources** is being unashamed to seek out the help you need regardless of the situation you may find yourself in. It is converting the knowledge, wisdom, and understanding acquired over a lifetime into the materials needed to construct a bridge that will get you over to your next level and prevent you from drowning. It is taking advantage of every opportunity to learn and grow utilizing all available means to enhance your life in all areas. Connections are **POWER**ful!

The **POWER of Prayer and Patience.** It is going deep within to connect with your higher being and making your requests known. It is casting your cares, fear, doubts, and uncertainties onto a force that can replace these things with peace. It is making time to just be still and be quiet, basking in the tranquility of the moment. It is freeing your mind, even if just for a small space in time, and permitting yourself to just be. It is about strengthening the connection with yourself. Prayer is **POWER**!

The **POWER of Forgiveness** is understanding the spiritual, physical, and emotional value of forgiveness of oneself and others. It is using the strength that you have built through trials, obstacles, and challenges to push through the threshold of unforgiveness and emerge victorious, healthy, and whole on the other side. It is choosing to view the transgressions that have been committed against you as bricks rather than stumbling blocks and stretching your heart to experience empathy and understanding. This releases your **POWER**!

The **POWER of Presence** is about being memorable and noteworthy, changing the temperature in any room that you step into. It is filling the room with a force so **POWER**ful that it is felt long after you are gone. It is as big as bringing an immediate hush over a crowd, or as simple as bringing someone a cup of coffee. It is being aware that eyes are always watching and ears are always listening, and governing yourself accordingly. Showing up is your **POWER**!

The **POWER of Self-Care** is recognizing that you are important and deserve to be taken care of by you. It is not feeling guilty for showing yourself the same love, compassion, and consideration that you show others. It is putting your air mask on first, ensuring that you are present, aware, and strong enough to assist and serve those placed within your charge. It is knowing and accepting that it is okay to step out of the light and into the shadows when needed to give your eyes a rest from staring into the sun and becoming blinded by the light. This is how you take back your **POWER**!

The POWER of You! is the irreplaceable gifts, talents, and breath of fresh air that you bring each time to set foot into any space. It is in the positive attention and respect that you command without saying a word. It is in the way that you carry yourself, your demeanor, your eyes, your smile, your voice, and all the little nuances that make you uniquely you. It is the joy, peace, and compassion that accompany you wherever you go, as well as those imperfections that make you perfectly imperfect. It is what makes you stand out from the crowd.

With these words, I leave you with the challenge of finding *The POWER of You!* It is there, way deep, deep, deep down inside, buried under years of misconception and misinformation. **Dig. Locate. Activate.** The world is waiting for you to manifest your **POWER**. Press toward the pentacle of your mountain. If that mountain presents itself as an obstacle, you have the **POWER** to command it to move. Let *The POWER of You!* awaken you, fuel your rocket, and blast you off into the next dimension of success! Remember, success is a decision. What decision are you going to make?

The POWER of You! is passing life's ultimate endurance test by proving you can go the distance. It is seeing opportunity in every situation and finding a situation for every opportunity. It is giving yourself the grace for the race. It is using every tool in your box to complete the mission. It is doing whatever it takes once the die is cast. No retreat, no surrender. This is *The POWER of You!!*

Ignite your Passion.

Define your Purpose.

Step into your POWER.

B Passionate.   B Purposeful.   B POWERful.

No one is YOU, and that is your POWER!

"True POWER is not pretending to be who you are not; it's admitting the truth of who you are."

~Suits

POWER
Quotes

"Once your mindset changes, everything on the outside will change along with it."

~Steve Maraboli

"Impossible is not a fact. It's an opinion."

~Muhammad Ali

"Difficulties do not come to destroy you, they come to help you realize your hidden potential and POWER."

~Bertina Power

"Purpose is how you use your experiences, talents, and gifts to better the lives of those around you."

~ Lindsay Peterson

"...and as we let our light shine, we unconsciously give other people permission to do the same."

~Marianne Williamson

"Death and life are in the power of the tongue..."

~ Proverbs 18:21, King James Version Bible

"Each of us has a gift or talent. We must individually tap into it in order to activate it."

~Bertina Power

"A man's gift maketh room for him, and bringeth him before great men."

~Holy Bible, KJV (Proverbs, 18:26)

"When your absence has the authority of presence, that is POWER."

~Harriet Rubin

"When every physical and mental resource is focused, one's POWER to solve a problem multiplies tremendously."

~Norman Vincent Peale

"Sometimes we don't know how strong we are until being strong is your only option."

~Unknown

"It is not selfish to love yourself, take care of yourself, and make your happiness a priority. It's necessary."

~Mandy Hale

"Prayer is the key in the morning and the bolt in the evening."

~Mahatma Ghandi

"The question isn't who is going to let me, it's who is going to stop me."

~Ayn Rand

"True POWER is not pretending to be who you are not; it's admitting the truth of who you are."

~Suits

"There is nothing on earth you cannot have - once you have mentally accepted the fact that you can have it."

~Robert Collier

"Without Pressure, we don't get Diamonds."

~Unknown

*"Coming back to where you started is not the
same as never leaving."*

~Terry Prachett

*"You have been criticizing yourself for years and it hasn't
worked. Try approving of yourself and see what
happens. "*

~Louise L. Hay

*"Be strong enough to stand alone, smart enough to know
when you need help and brave enough to ask for help."*

~Unknown

*"PAIN helps create our PURPOSE.
Turn PAIN into POWER!"*
~Bertina Power

*"If you don't demonstrate respect for your time,
you can be sure no one else will."*
~ Chuck Cusson

*"If you look closely,
most overnight successes took a long time."*
~ Steve Jobs

*"Respect yourself enough to walk away from
ANYTHING that no longer serves you,
grows you or makes you happy."*
~ Unknown

*"I'm thankful for my struggle because without it I
wouldn't have stumbled across my strength!"*
~ Alex Elle

"Sometimes God takes you on a journey you didn't know
you needed to bring you everything you ever wanted.
Trust the plan."
~Unknown

*"The struggle you're in today is developing the
strength you need for tomorrow."*
~ Unknown

*"Your destination doesn't change because
your mission was disrupted."*
~ Byron Nelson

*"Everything that is faced can't be changed but nothing
can be changed until it is faced."*
~ James Baldwin

"Never give up, for that is just the place and time that the tide will turn."
~ Harriet Beecher Stowe

"Nothing is impossible, the word itself says I'm possible."
~ Audrey Hepburn

POWER
Sources

Thank you for accompanying me along this journey to finding your **POWER**. I would love to share with you some of the reading materials that have been a source of **POWER** for me. It is my hope that you will find a light in them as I did, and that the words between the pages will illuminate your path and **POWER** for years to come.

1. *Holy Bible*, King James Version
2. *The Secret* by Rhonda Byrne
3. *Automatic Millionaire* by David Bach
4. *The Best Year Ever* by Michael S. Hyatt
5. *Becoming* by Michelle Obama
6. *What I Know For Sure* by Oprah Winfrey
7. *You are a Badass* by Jen Sincero
8. *Getting Past What You'll Never Get Over* by John F. Westfall
9. *Rich Dad, Poor Dad* by Robert Kiyosaki
10. *Good To Great* by Jim Collins
11. *Letters To A Young Brother* by Hill Harper
12. *Act Like A Lady, Think Like A Man* by Steve Harvey
13. *I Know Why the Caged Bird Sings* by Maya Angelou
14. *Reposition Yourself* by T.D. Jakes

15. *Yesterday, I Cried* by Iyanla Vanzant
16. *Their Eyes Are Watching God* by Zora Neal Hurston
17. *Who Moved My Cheese* by Spencer Johnson, MD
18. *Are You Out There, God* by Sis. Mary Rose McGeady
19. *The Book of Success*, Edited by Richard Shea
20. *The Power of Goals*, Compiled by Katherine Karvelas

About the
AUTHOR

Bertina M. Power is an author, motivational speaker, real estate broker, general contractor, investor, and coach. Her exposure and life experience has afforded her the opportunity to appear on HGTV programs *Designed to Sell, My House is Worth What?, and National Open House, as well as the Steve Harvey Show.*

Bertina is the oldest of four children, a proud native Chicagoan, and is the President and CEO of Queen B Media, Inc. She is the author of the prolific yet practical guide to accessing and releasing the true **POWER** within entitled *"The POWER of You!"* Bertina unveils the necessary actions that encourage personal success and growth.

She helps others release 'stifling beliefs' so they are no longer confined by internal or external barriers. Her larger-than-life presence exudes confidence, authenticity, fearlessness, and of course, **POWER** to everyone she encounters.

Bertina has served in leadership positions, such as President, Vice-President, Treasurer, Sergeant-at-Arms, and other leadership roles in various organizations. Bertina is a woman of many talents and wears many hats, managing her numerous accomplishments with courage, grace, and perseverance. Her leadership qualities, combined with her interpersonal skills, personal values, and clear goals, have been the catapult for her advancement to where she is today.

Bertina is also the Founder and President of Queen B Consulting, LLC and CEO of Queen B Construction & Rehab, Inc. She is a professional Real Estate consultant with over 20 years of real estate experience and new construction sales experience. Bertina is a trusted advisor in the urban real estate markets. She also coaches business professionals as a *Success Specialist* and is a highly sought-after coach.

Bertina graduated Magna Cum Laude from one of the oldest HBCU's, Hampton University in Hampton, Virginia, and received a Bachelor of Science in Accounting. She has two sons, Brandon and Haydon. In December 2017, she partnered with the Educational Advancement Fund (EAF) to establish a scholarship endowment fund in honor of her youngest son, who has severe cerebral palsy. This partnership will provide scholarships to students with special needs who seek to excel in higher education. A percentage of all book sales will go toward funding this scholarship.

Besides spending time with her sons, family, and friends, Bertina also loves to play tennis, swim, ride horses, and travel; she has visited such exotic locations such as Paris, London, and Ghana, West Africa.

Whether business or community involvement, her goal is to leave a *"Legacy of Leadership"* wherever she goes. Bertina says her philosophy on life and what keeps her going is an abiding belief that her work truly helps people and that no one is you, and that is your **POWER!**

CPSIA information can be obtained
at www.ICGtesting.com
Printed in the USA
JSHW020438310123
37104JS00004B/24